Introduction

In the course of the nineteenth century, during the expansion of their overseas empire, the French were the most prolific users of river gunboats, deploying them worldwide, from the jungles of South America to the desert near Timbuctoo. In Africa the Marchand expedition hauled a small river gunboat across the continent from West to East, through mountain ranges, jungles and swamps, and launched her on the upper Nile near an abandoned Egyptian fort at a place called Fashoda. In Indochina, the rivers offered a means of projecting power well into the interior, and at one spot on the Mekong, the French even constructed a light railway line to transport gunboats up-river past a series of rapids.

When France attempted to re-establish her hegemony in Indochina after the collapse of Imperial Japan in 1945, she was faced with a major insurrection by nationalists. In the dramatic conflict which ensued the French lost heavily in many local reverses, culminating in the catastrophe of Diên Biên Fu. In complete contrast to the disasters which befell them on land, on the river systems the French held the upper hand. The French Navy had been involved from the outset, their principal role being the transportation by water of assault groups to retake key towns. The introduction of these *Divisions navales d'assaut* (usually known as *Dinassaut*) cemented French control over the extensive waterways. A total of ten *Dinassaut* units were eventually formed, two of which were later transferred to the South Vietnamese Navy when the French gave up the struggle. There were also many patrol units manned by the Army, much of their personnel being drawn from the armoured forces.

After four years of German occupation of mainland France, the French had to rely heavily on their wartime allies for equipment, and they were forced to improvise many types of riverine combat vessels, armed with whatever weapons came to hand.

After they left Indochina, the types which the French evolved were passed on to the South Vietnamese, who in turn relied heavily on American support. When the United States made the fateful decision to greatly expand its presence in Vietnam, the Americans copied many of the existing French conversions, and went on to develop their own riverine combat vessels, with varying degrees of success. One can therefore trace a continuous line of development from the French improvisations of the 1940s to the final American designs of 1975.

We will examine the wealth of models available in various scales, from 1:76 to 1:35. As with the early French craft, we can modify several models of landing craft to serve as armed and armoured patrol vessels and monitors, and this process continues into the US period. With its vast industrial base, the United States was able to develop many purpose-built craft, and the last of the river monitors were formidable vessels, with flamethrowers and even water cannons. The story winds up with the last of the 'river destroyers', the special ASPB prototype built by Sikorsky, too late to take part in the Vietnam conflict, but which continued in use by US Special Forces for several years. The Author is scratch-building this beauty in 1:35 scale – see his Website for details.

Many of the photos, both French and American, are reproduced from snapshots taken by individual soldiers and sailors. Their rarity and relevance outweigh their less-than-professional quality. Similarly, the vast range of conversions means that the plans must be regarded as typical of a specific type based on photographic evidence, but many variations of armour and armament could and did exist, as noted in the historical introduction and also the Models Section.

Below: *LCG-111*, an ex-British LCG(M). note the two 25-pounder guns forward and a 40mm Bofors on top of the superstructure aft.

Right: *LCI-263* with a 75mm APX cannon in the bow gun tub. This particular vessel would be sunk by a mine on 27 September 1953. Inset is an example of a typical unit badge worn by LCI crewmen.

THE BEGINNINGS – FRENCH CONVERSIONS

In 1945 the French Navy and Army searched around for whatever shallow-draught landing craft were available in the Far East, left over from the Second World War. The British supplied the slow and vulnerable LCA (Landing Craft Assault), armed only with Lewis guns, but the French were so desperate they accepted anything which could float. A 1:72 scale model of an LCA is available from Mach 2 in their 'Armageddon' range.

In addition to the LCAs, they found two wooden-hulled armoured Landing Craft Support (Medium), the **LCS(M) Mk III**. These had been disarmed but they still mounted an electrically-operated turret which could accept twin .30 calibre machine guns. Later a pair of .50 cal Brownings may have been installed. The well in front of the bridge designed to house a 4in smoke mortar could well have been

■ LANDING CRAFT SUPPORT MK III

Launched: From early 1942, by Thornycroft.

Dimensions: Displacement 13.3 tons; Length 12.7m / 41ft 8in; Beam 3m / 10ft; Draught 0.68m / 2ft 3in.

Crew: 11.

Power/Speed: Twin screws; 2 x Ford V8 65bhp petrol engines / 10 knots.

Guns/Armour: 2 x MGs (.30 cal Brownings probably replaced by .50 cal Brownings); 1 x 60mm mortar / Bullet-proof plating to wooden hull sides and to bridge and turret.

Below: An official drawing of a LCS(M) Mk III as built for Royal Navy service.

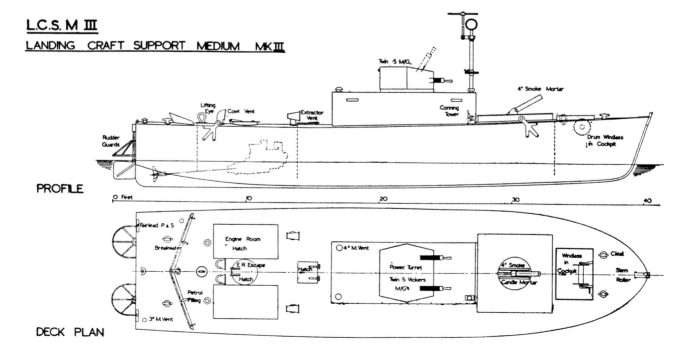

■ LANDING CRAFT GUN (MEDIUM)

Launched: June 1944 by Tyne Tees.

Dimensions: Displacement 270 tons (380 tons full load); Length: 47m / 154ft 6in; Beam: 6.8m / 22ft 4in; Draught: 1.7m / 5ft 6in.

Crew: 2 officers + 25 men.

Power/Speed: Twin screws; Paxman Diesel engines 1000bhp / 11.75–13.5 knots.

Guns/Armour: 2 x 25-pounder (87.6mm, 3.45in) gun/howitzers; 1 x 40mm Bofors; 2 x 20mm Oerlikons; 2 x .50 cal MGs / 25mm NC sides and bridge; 12.7mm NC on deck over engines and magazine; 15-lb plating to gun turrets and conning tower.

Landing Craft Gun (Medium) *LCG-111* as modified for French service. *(Drawing by the Author)*

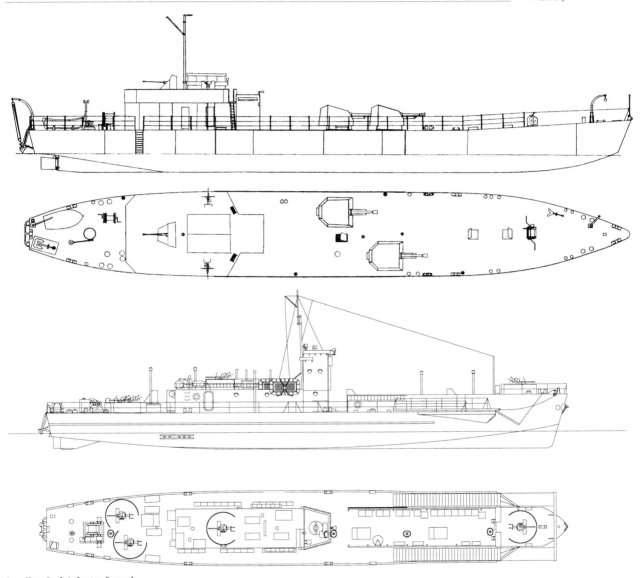

Landing Craft Infantry (Large)
Early US variant with tall square bridge and side ramps
(All uncredited drawings © George Richardson)

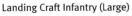

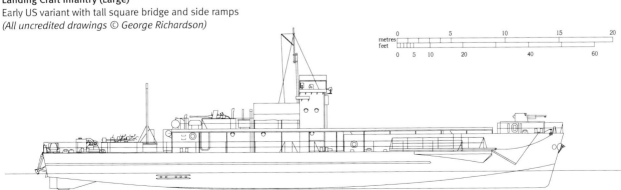

Landing Craft Infantry (Large)
French *LCI-101*

Landing Craft Infantry (Large)
US version with round bridge and side ramps

metres	0		5		10		15		20
feet	0	5	10		20		40		60

Landing Craft Infantry (Large)
US version with round bridge and bow ramp

Landing Craft Infantry (Large)
Ex-US *LCI-1092* as French LSSL *L-9032*, September 1951

metres	0		5		10		15		20
feet	0	5	10		20		40		60

used to mount a 60mm French mortar. Named *Vivandière* and *Tonkinoise II*, these wooden craft were used by the French between early 1946 and October 1947, when they disappeared from the inventory. For a photo, see the Models Section.

The British also supplied heavier landing craft, plus a small armoured Monitor, a Landing Craft Gun (Medium). Designated *LCG-111*, she was armed with two 25-pounder field guns, which must have caused severe ammunition supply problems, as they were the only weapons of this calibre in Indochina. Designated as gun/howitzers, they did however have the ability to lob shells into riverside trenches and foxholes. To back up the 25-pounders in this role she also carried a French 120mm mortar, of the type which would be fitted in the central well of the LCM-6s converted to Monitors. As no kit of the LCG (M) yet exists, a model would have to be completely scratch-built, so no further details are given here.

For their part, the Americans transferred to the French Navy a number of Landing Craft Infantry (Large). Built in quantity during the war, the **LCI(L)** had been designed to carry a second wave of infantry to the beaches in amphibious operations, and in Indochina they were used to transport troops to combat zones. There were a number of variants of the basic design (see drawings), and the French Navy added additional armament to lay down suppressive fire.

The LCIs, which had seen much action in the Second World War were quite worn out by 1950, when they began to be replaced by **LSSLs** (Landing Ship Support Large), nine of which were transferred to France by the US Navy from August 1950 and given the names *Arbalète, Arquebuse, Hallebarde, Javeline, Pertuisane, La Rapière, Etendard, Framée* and *Oriflamme*. Derived from the LCI, with which they shared the same hull, the LSSLs were known as 'river cruisers' because of their heavy armament. Note the differences between the first six and the last three

Top: The heavily-armed LSSLs, modified from the LCI, were often employed to control *Dinassaut* units. The last three exchanged their forward 3in/50 for a single Bofors, which allowed them to deploy launchers for 12 shore bombardment rockets.

Above: A former French LSSL as handed over to the South Vietnamese Navy.

■ LANDING CRAFT INFANTRY (LARGE)

Launched: 1943 onwards, by various builders.

Dimensions: Displacement 380 tons; Length 48.7m / 159ft 9in; Beam 7.2m / 23ft 7in; Draught 1.8m / 5ft 11in.

Crew: 3 officers + 55 men.

Power/Speed: Twin screws; 8 x Gray Marine 8V 71 Diesel engines 1320bhp / 16 knots.

Guns/Armour: Various combinations of 75mm APX, 3in/50, 40mm Bofors, 20mm Oerlikon or MG151, machine guns/ Armour plate around bridge plus gun shields.

■ LANDING SHIP SUPPORT LARGE

Launched: 1944 onwards, by various builders.

Dimensions: Displacement 390 tons; Length 48.7m / 159ft 9in; Beam 7.2m / 23ft 7in; Draught 1.8m / 5ft 11in.

Crew: 3 officers + 55 men.

Power/Speed: Twin screws; 8 x Gray Marine 8V 71 Diesel engines 1320bhp / 16 knots.

Guns/Armour: First six: 1 x 3in/50; 2 x twin 40mm Bofors; 4 x 20mm Oerlikons; 2 x .30 cal MGs; 2 x 81mm mortars / Bullet-proof plating to bridge, conning tower and radio room. Armament on last three: 2 x twin 40mm Bofors; 1 x single Bofors; 4 x 20mm Oerlikons; 2 x .30 cal MGs; 2 x 81mm mortars; 2 x 6-round BRR rocket launchers.

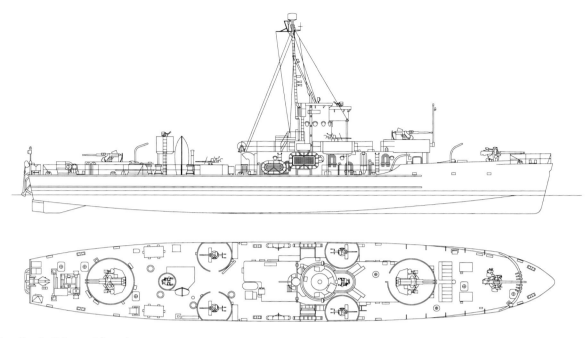

Landing Craft Support (Large)
US version as built

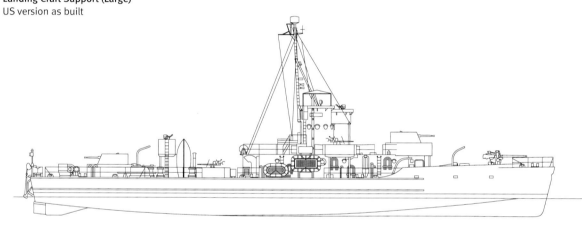

Landing Craft Support (Large)
French *LSSL-1*, December 1950

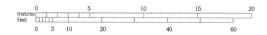

Right: Gressier barge *Tonnerre* (ex-*Foudre*) showing her twin 13.2mm Hotchkiss machine gun forward mount, armoured conning tower, bridge wings and bulwarks. A Bren Gun is mounted on the roof over the conning tower.

Left: Bow view of an armoured LCVP.

Left: One of the requisitioned Gressier barges as armed and armoured. Note the cylindrical conning tower, the bulwarks of armour plate, and the twin13.2mm mounting on the fore deck.

outlined in the table. They were often used in support of *Dinassaut* operations as they possessed extensive command and control facilities. As with the British **LCG(M)**, the LSSL was originally developed to provide gunfire support to beach landings, under the wartime designation of LCS(L).

Before the introduction of the Monitors converted from LCM-6s, heavy firepower was provided by **Gressier barges** converted to 'river battleships' (although colloquially known as 'rice-paddy battleships'). These were commercial rice-transport barges, hastily armoured, and armed with a range of weapons up to 75mm APX cannons, plus left-over Japanese 13.2mm and 25mm AA guns. They were fitted with wooden accommodation for troops, but habitability was compromised by the lack of any toilet facilities on board. They were also very slow and unmanoeuvrable but they proved useful stopgaps until more modern vessels became available.

By March 1946 there were six of them, named *Dévastation*, *Lave*, *Tonnante*, *Foudre*, *Volcon* and *Terreur*. *Lave* was sunk

■ GRESSIER BARGE

Launched: Converted between late 1945 and late 1947 by BMEO Workshops & Saigon Arsenal.

Dimensions: Displacement 220 tons; Length 31.5m / 103ft 4in; Beam 6.5m / 21ft 4in: Draught 1.1m to 1.8m / 3ft 7in to 5ft 11in.

Crew: 14, plus up to a company of troops for 2-3 day operations, or 250 men over short distance.

Power/Speed: Single screw; 1 x single cylinder Bolinder hot-bulb semi-diesel engine 25bhp to 45bhp / 5 to 7 knots.

Guns/Armour: (Typical) 2 x 25mm Japanese Type 96; 1 x twin 13.2mm Hotchkiss HMGs; 3 or 4 x .30 cal Browning MGs; 1 x 81mm mortar / Bullet-proof conning tower and side bulwarks. *Foudre* armament: 1 x 75mm Model 1897 QF; 4 x 25mm Model 96 cannons, (1 twin + 2 single); 1 x twin 13.2mm Hotchkiss HMGs; 2 x 8mm Hotchkiss MGs; 2 x .30 cal Browning MGs; 2 x 81mm mortars; 1 x 50mm mortar.

by a mine in June 1947 and replaced by another requisitioned as *Lave II*, but the remainder – apart from *Tonnerre* (*Foudre* renamed) – were handed back to the Gressier concern by 1952 to continue transporting rice. *Tonnerre* was still in service in 1954 when the French withdrew from Indochina. One of these would make an interesting model, but again it would have to be scratch-built.

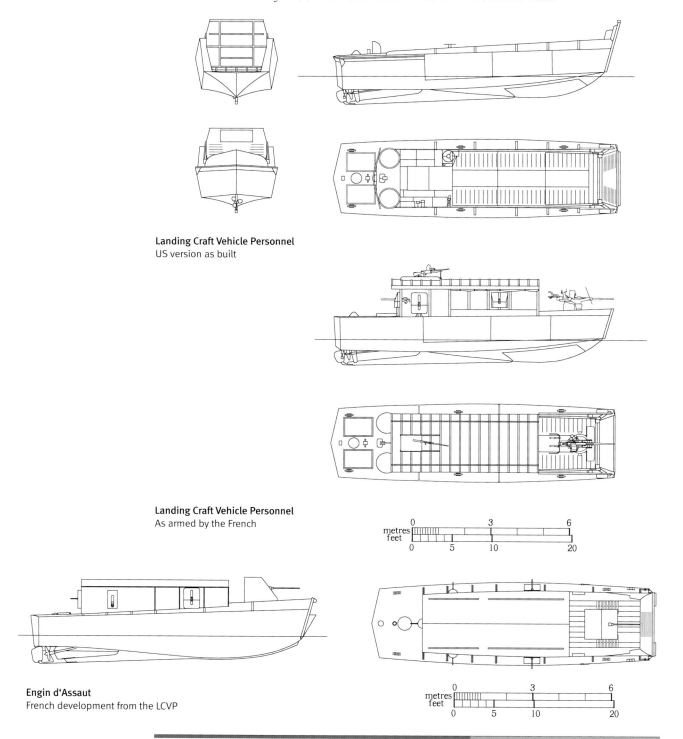

Landing Craft Vehicle Personnel
US version as built

Landing Craft Vehicle Personnel
As armed by the French

Engin d'Assaut
French development from the LCVP

■ LANDING CRAFT VEHICLE PERSONNEL

Launched: Built during the war; converted late 1940s.

Dimensions: Displacement 7 tons; Length 10.97m / 36ft; Beam 3.18m / 10ft 5in; Draught 1.09m to 1.15m / 3ft 7in to 3ft 9in.

Crew: 6 + 10 troops.

Power/Speed: Single screw; 1 x Gray 64HN9 Marine Diesel 225bhp / 7 knots.

Guns/Armour: 1 x 20mm Oerlikon; 2 x .30 cal Browning MGs; 2 x 7.5mm MAC 31 MGs OR 2 x FM 24/29 LMGs; 2 x VB grenade launchers (7.5mm MAS 36 rifles in cradles) or 2 x PIAT; at least one LCVP was armed with a twin Japanese 13.2mm Hotchkiss HMG mounting forward / Bullet-proof (7mm) gun shields, bow plate and side panels.

The principal small vessels armed by the French fell into two categories. The first of these comprised the conversions of the American 'Higgins Boat', the standard **LCVP** (Landing Craft Vehicle Personnel), which had served in their thousands during the Second World War.

The French added extra armour plates to the old American LCVPs, built of wood, which were already protected by two plates

■ *ENGIN D'ASSAUT*

Launched: Beginning in 1950, by Cherbourg Dockyard.

Dimensions: Displacement 10 tons; Length 10.75m / 35ft 3in; Beam 3.23m / 10ft 7in; Draught 0.95m to 1.15m / 3ft 1in to 3ft 9in.

Crew: 6 + up to 10 troops.

Power/Speed: Single screw; 1 x Gray 64HN9 Marine Diesel 225bhp / 7 knots.

Guns/Armour: 1 x 20mm MG151 cannon; 2 x .30 cal Browning MGs; 2 x 7.5mm MAC 31 MGs OR 2 x FM 24/29 LMGs; 2 x VB grenade launchers (7.5mm MAS 36 rifles in cradles) / Bullet-proof (7mm) gun shields, bow plate and side panels.

Below: A pair of EA (*Engin d'Assaut*) from *Dinassaut 8* on the Bassac River in the region of Can Tho. This photo has often been shown reversed, but on the original one can discern the number '59' on the roof of the nearer EA. *(Photo ECPA)*

Left: An 8-metre FOM taking on ammunition in the form of 'camembert' ammunition drums for the MAC 31 machine gun. The small size of the craft is apparent. *(Photo Lieutenant Colonel Hubert Tourret, by kind permission of Mme Tourret)*

Many of the drawings, particularly the French boats and conversions of US craft, are highly speculative. Many of these modifications were 'field conversions' so no records were kept. Some drawings of purpose designed boats have been lost. Should any readers have any original documentation of US or French vessels please contact the publisher so the artwork can be corrected as necessary.

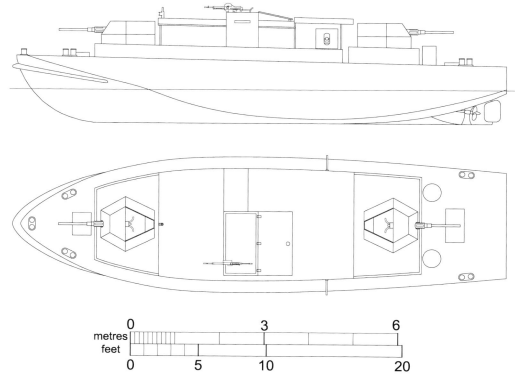

metres 0 3 6
feet 0 5 10 20

French 11-metre FOM

Above: 11-metre FOM of the 4th Dragoons in Cochinchina. Note the straight deck line compared with the later STCAN RAG Boat version. *(Photo ECPA)*

Right: The popular twin-shaft 11-metre FOM. Note the cramped shield fitted to the bow .50 cal. A second identical mounting was fitted at the stern. *(Photo Lieutenant Colonel Hubert Tourret, by kind permission of Mme Tourret)*

bolted on to each hull side. They were armed with a 20mm Oerlikon, machine guns, rifle grenade launchers or even PIATs. As gunboats, the opening bow landing ramp was replaced by a fixed armour plate, as the weight of the Oerlikon made them trim horizontally compared with the bow-up attitude as built. Opening a bow ramp would have swamped and sunk them. They were reliable, but very slow, and extremely noisy.

Cherbourg Dockyard built a steel version of the LCVP as the EA or **Engin d'Assaut**, with the Oerlikon replaced by the lighter and more effective German MG151 20mm cannon. The EA retained the trim of the original LCVP, so it appears that the

Left: A close-up view of the forward gun mounting on an 11-metre FOM. Note the navigation lights mounted on top of the canopy behind the gunner. The weapon in the shield is not a .50 cal Browning, and is probably a 20mm Oerlikon – which would leave very little room inside the gun shield.

■ 11-METRE FOM

Launched: 1949 on.

Dimensions: Displacement 12 tons; Length 11m / 36ft 1in; Beam 3m / 9ft 10in; Draught 1.1m / 3ft 7in.

Crew: 7-8.

Power/Speed: Twin screws; 2 x Renault 70bhp Diesel engines / 11 knots.

Guns/Armour: 2 x .50 cal Browning HMGs; OR 1 x .50 cal HMG + 1 x 60mm mortar; 4 x 7.5mm MAC 31 MGs; 2 x VB grenade launchers (7.5mm MAS 36 rifles in cradles); 75mm recoilless rifle / Bullet-proof armour: waterline belt, .50 cal shields fore and aft, MG shields and around steering position.

bow ramp was once more able to lower. As these craft were powered by a single diesel engine, in photos they can often be seen coupled side-by-side in pairs to avoid being immobilised by the loss of one engine. Steering these pairs in narrow confines must have been demanding.

To supplant and eventually replace the slow and noisy LCVP/EA types, the French conceived a new armoured vessel, the 8-metre FOM (standing for *France d'Outre-Mer*, or France Overseas) with one diesel engine. They were not converted from existing landing craft but were completely new builds, designed in 1949 with help from the French Navy. They had an armoured belt above the waterline and all-round protection for the steering position. Armed with various machine guns and two grenade launchers, they drew only 80cm (2ft 7in) of water and were popular with the armoured forces who operated them. However, they were relatively slow and noisy, and the single rudder gave them a large turning circle, so a larger version, the **11-metre FOM**, was introduced, with twin propellers and twin rudders. They were more heavily armed, but the draught increased to 1.1m (3ft 7in).

In turn an even longer version would be built by STCAN, which would survive into South Vietnamese service as the RAG (or River Assault Group) Boat.

Another type of small landing craft conversion was based on the LCPL (Landing Craft Personnel Large). The French used armed versions, both armoured and unarmoured, designated as ***Vedettes Vietnamiennes***. The two original bow machine gun positions were blanked off in both versions.

Another French development was the use of American LVT Alligators as support gunboats for troop deployment in the rice paddies, and there are photos of them cruising the river systems. They were operated by the Légionnaires of the 1er REC (*Premier Régiment Étranger de Chars*).

■ *VEDETTE VIETNAMIENNE*

Launched: During the Second World War as LCPLs

Dimensions: Displacement 6.5 tons; Length 11.07m / 36ft 4in; Beam 3.3m / 10ft 10in; Draught 1.1m / 3ft 7in.

Power/Speed: Single screw; Gray 64HN9 Marine Diesel 225bhp / 8 knots.

Guns/Armour: 1 x 20mm MG151 or .50 cal Browning MG in bullet-proof shield. Unarmoured boats: 2 x .303in Bren Guns. Armoured boats: 3 x .30 cal Browning MGs / Bullet-proof hull side plating, cabin and roof.

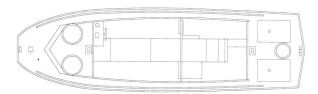

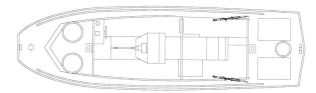

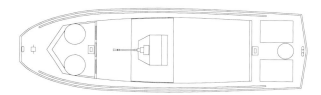

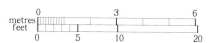

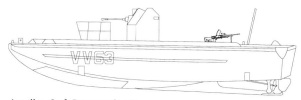

Landing Craft Personnel Large
Original US wartime version

Landing Craft Personnel Large
French conversion to unarmoured *Vedette Vietnamienne*

Landing Craft Personnel Large
French conversion to armoured *Vedette Vietnamienne*

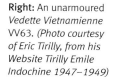

Right: An unarmoured
Vedette Vietnamienne
VV63. *(Photo courtesy
of Eric Tirilly, from his
Website Tirilly Emile
Indochine 1947–1949)*

Below: Armoured
Vedette Vietnamienne
VV51 at Vinh Long in
1948. *(Photo courtesy
of Eric Tirilly, from his
Website Tirilly Emile
Indochine 1947–1949)*

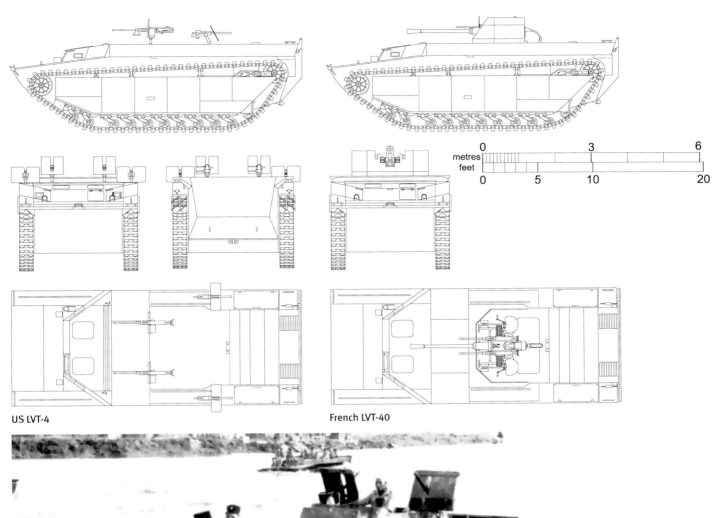

US LVT-4

French LVT-40

Left: Cruising the Red River is an LVT(A)-5, the close support version armed with the turret and howitzer from the M5 light tank, crewed by the *1er REC*. Note the rails around the turret to limit the depression of the main gun, and the anti-swamping shield at the rear.

Left: An LVT-40 of *1er REM*.

■ LVT-4 / LVT-40 / LVT(A)-5

Dimensions: 16.5 tonnes empty + weight of Bofors, gunshield and ammunition; Length 7.97m / 26ft 1¾in; Width 3.25m / 10ft 8in; Height (ex-gunshield) 3.70m / 12ft 1⅖in.

Power/Speed: Water propulsion and steering by cleated tracks; Motor 250bhp 7-cylinder Continental W 670-9A radial; Speed 18mph / 30kph (on land); 7½mph / 12kph (in water).

Crew: Driver, radioman, 2 Bofors gunners, 2-3 Bofors loaders (LVT-40).

Guns/Armour: LVT-4: various machine guns on pintle mounts plus recoilless rifles. LVT(A)-5: 1 x 75mm howitzer, 1 x bow-mounted .30 cal Browning; 2 x pintle mounts on turret for .30 cal Brownings / 7-25mm armour. LVT-40: 1 x 40mm Bofors; 2 x co-axial .50 cal Brownings / 7-25mm armour.

Although these amphibious armoured vehicles drew more water than the landing craft previously noted, this was never a handicap. Propelled by their tracks, they could navigate practically everywhere in the main rivers, tributaries and rice paddies.

The **LVT-40** was a local conversion of the standard troop carrier Alligator, armed with a 40mm Bofors and twin .50 cal Brownings in an angular shield. Conceived by Capitaine De La Capelle of the *1er Chasseurs*, at least two were used in a fire-

Right: A French LCM-6 conversion to a Monitor with a new bow and Coventry armoured car turret. Note the substantial collision mat, and the crewman's pet climbing the antenna on the left. *(Photo ECPA T52.106.64)*

Right: Initially, the Monitors mounted a fixed crow's nest carrying an observer, to spy out concealed enemy positions on the riverbank. However, in combat the casualty rate of the observers was so high that the fixed crow's nest was quickly abandoned. In later conversions supplied to the South Vietnamese by the Americans, some Monitors and Command Boats had a retractable crow's nest.

Left: An LCM-6 converted to a Monitor. *(Photo ECPA)*

■ LCM-6 MONITOR CONVERSION

Launched: Late Second World War, by various builders.

Dimensions: Displacement 47 tons; Length 17.26m / 56ft 7in; Beam 4.28m / 14ft; Draught 1.22m / 4ft.

Power/Speed: Twin screws; 2 x Gray 64HN9 Marine Diesels, total 330bhp / 8 knots.

Guns/Armour: In front turret: 1 x 2-pounder QF; 1 x 20mm MG151; On rear deck: 1 x 20mm MG151 + 2 x .50 cal Browning HMGs; Central well: 120mm mortar; 4 x MAS 36 rifles in cradles for grenade launching / 15mm bullet-proof plating on hull sides and bridge; Original Coventry turret armour upgraded by spaced armour plates.

Below: LCM-6 fitted by the French with extra armour and armament: the enclosed shields mount 20mm MG151 cannons or .50 cal Brownings, the vertical shields Bren Guns or even PIATs. *(Photo NHHC 79374)*

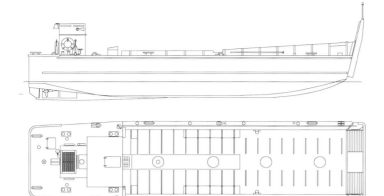

Landing Craft Mechanised
US LCM-6 mod 2

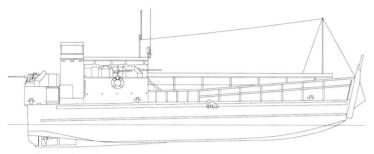

Landing Craft Mechanised
French armed and armoured conversion

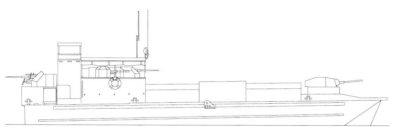

Landing Craft Mechanised
French Monitor conversion

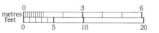

Close-up view of the mortar muzzle and sight, and a mount for a cut-down MAS 36 rifle, for firing rifle grenades.

support role in Indochina. Based on early model LVT-4s, they were named *Le Tonnant* and *Le Foudroyant*. Similar Bofors conversions of late-model LVT-4s, with the bow .30 cal Browning but no co-axial .50 cal Brownings, were used during the landings at Suez in 1956.

The French made extensive use of larger landing craft such as the LCM-3 and its longer version the **LCM-6**. Many of these were up-armoured and armed, but in addition the French began the construction of specific Monitors, by deleting the bow ramp of the LCM-6 and welding on a solid prow section, complete with the turret from a Coventry armoured car on an armour glacis. This turret retained the old British 2-pounder main gun, which was virtually useless, as it could only fire the solid 40mm AT round. A HE round was developed for it by the British Army but never issued. To increase its firepower, the co-axial 7.92mm BESA was replaced by a 20mm MG151. Also note the spaced armour fitted to the turret in the photos on pages 14 and 15.

The Americans would continue this type of conversion, supplying Bofors-armed Monitors to the South Vietnamese, before developing the LCM-6 into their own specific river Monitors, with greatly improved hull and superstructure protection.

Above: The120mm mortar of the type which was mounted in the well deck of Monitors.

Right: An up-armoured and armed LCM-6, showing the firing cuts in the bow door and side armour. *(Photo NHHC 79379)*

Model Products

'Box Scale'

LINDBERG LCI
1:150 Scale

Can be built out-of-the-box and re-armed 'à la française'. With some work the same kit can be converted to an LSSL, which shared the same basic hull design. This old re-issued kit turns out to be very close to the recently introduced 1:144 scale for ship and submarine models. Photo-etch and detail parts for these may therefore be suitable, and Shapeways can supply 3D-printed crewmen.

REVELL (REF H435) *ASHEVILLE* CLASS GUNBOAT
1:131 Scale

The kit was originally released in the 1960s as class leader USS *Asheville*. The kit has been reissued by Revell Germany as USS *Defiance*, now quoted as 1:131 scale. The bump on the 3in turret should be a perspex dome, and the kit has vastly oversized rail stanchions. The odd box-scale Revell kit size means that the closest suitable photo-etch would be Tom's Modelworks Etched Brass set Ref T-144-5, which provides the 2-bar and 3-bar railings required for the *Asheville* class. This is a good basic kit of an attractive vessel, which lends itself to upgrading.

1:76 & 1:72 Scales

These can be considered together, as both scales are very close. Only measuring with a ruler could differentiate between them at close range.

DRAGON (REF 7389) BUFFALO & ZVEZDA (REF 61704) 40mm BOFORS FOR CONVERSION TO LVT-40
1:72 Scale

The old Airfix Buffalo kit was under-sized. A much better base is the modern 1:72 scale Dragon version, plus Zvezda's 1:72 scale Bofors.

MILICAST (REF LCM6W) + (REF BB175) FOR CONVERSION TO FRENCH MONITOR
1:76 Scale

■ The basic LCM-6 hull which will be substantially modified. The Coventry kit supplies the turret and turret hatches, and the tyres for mooring fenders.

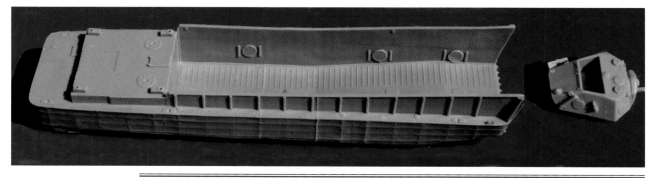

MILICAST (REF LCPLUSW) FOR CONVERSION TO VEDETTE VIETNAMIENNE
1:76 Scale

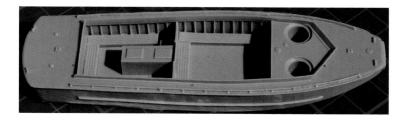

■ Milicast also produces a very large model of the LCI(L), perfect for conversion to the armed French Indochina version. The masters were produced by Dan Taylor, and the resin with brass etch kit builds into an impressive model no less than 650mm long.

DRAGON (REF 7388) LVT-(A)4
1:72 Scale

■ The Dragon kit makes a perfect companion for the smaller scale LVT-40 conversion. The track units fix to a one-piece main hull section. For the French version in Indochina the ring mounting and single .50 cal should be replaced by a pair of side-mounted .30 cal Brownings behind small shields.

AIRFIX (REF AO2340) HIGGINS LCVP FOR CONVERSION TO FRENCH PATROL GUNBOAT
1:72 Scale

■ A full-hull detailed model. To convert to an all-steel EA will require some work, as Airfix have moulded all the wood stringers on the interior of the side plates, with armour panels bolted to the exterior. The best option is to produce an armed and armoured LCVP. The bow ramp lowering gear should be discarded, as the replacement armour plate was welded in place.

SKYTREX FIREFIGHT 20 SERIES

■ These 1:76 scale high-quality cast resin and white metal waterline kits are intended for wargamers, which means that they are relatively sturdy. It also means they are a fine base for adding details. The photos are publicity shots of completed models, courtesy of Skytrex.

SKYTREX (REF FF020) AMERICAN PROGRAM 4 MONITOR
1:76 Scale

■ The kit comes with an alternative canvas canopy for the central well, replacing the mortar mounting, to represent a CCB (Command & Control Boat). The waterline hull, superstructure and MG turrets are a one-piece resin casting, with separate resin Bofors shield and 20mm turret, and white metal castings for the guns, stern winch, radome and fenders.

On the Monitor and ATC, the bar armour is represented by simple rectangular section mouldings on the hull sides. More seriously, the bar armour around the superstructure is simply moulded against the superstructure plates, whereas on the real Monitor it stood some distance away. Also there is no bar armour protection around the coxwain's position. Careful sanding or scraping of the horizontal runs of the hull bars can render them less rectangular. Rectifying the lack of offset around the superstructure will involve cutting or filing off the bar armour sections to reduce the size of the superstructure, and replacing them with plastic rod or wire. A modeller not wishing to go to such

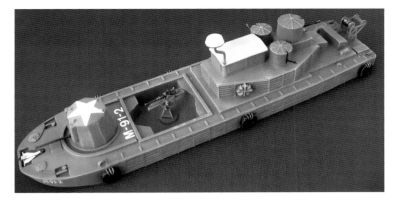

extremes can paint the interior walls to represent the empty ration cans or ammo boxes placed there by the crew in the pious hope of increasing the protection – see the 'Zippo' in the Modelmakers' Showcase on page 48.

The Mk 2 81mm mortar in the well deck of the Program 4 Monitors was the Mod 0. It was not fitted with the piggy-back .50 cal Browning of the Mk 2 Mod 1, which should be omitted.

SKYTREX (REF FF021) ATC WITH BOW RAMP FOR CONVERSION TO DOUCHE
1:76 Scale

■ For details of this unique conversion, see page 55.

SKYTREX (REF FF022) PROGRAM 4 ASPB EARLY VERSION
1:76 Scale

■ The bow turret is armed with twin .50 cal Brownings and the top turret with a 20mm cannon. For the Mk I the rear 40mm Mk 18 and .30 cal were not fitted. For wargaming the railings and steps are moulded solid. For a display or diorama model these can be cut off and replaced with wire or stretched sprue. Otherwise, the quality of the castings is excellent.

SKYTREX (REF FF023) PROGRAM 4 ASPB LATE VERSION
1:76 Scale

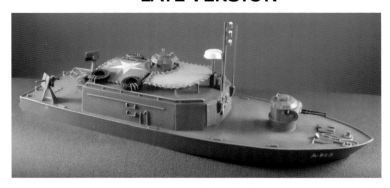

The Mk II with the rear deck well plated over and the combined mortar and MG removed. The tripod-mounted MGs are correctly represented as .30 cal Brownings. On both versions, the projections around the turret tops are actually armoured glass vision blocks and can be painted accordingly.

SKYTREX (REF FF024) SOUTH VIETNAMESE RPC
1:76 Scale

Similar comments apply to this small but well-cast vessel. One odd feature is the moulding of the gunners inside their armoured cupolas. One detail omitted is the canopy and its supports.

MACH 2 ARMAGEDDON KIT (REF AR 06) VIETNAM PATROL BOAT PBR 31 Mk II 'PIBBER'
1:72 Scale

Mach 2 of France produce a limited-run injection kit of the PBR Mk II, complete with a four-man crew. As with their aircraft kits, the PBR will need some

work to produce a realistic model, notably in correcting mould problems with the hull bottom (raised bumps, a hole near the bows and soft angles), the armament (crude M60s and M16s, rear Browning lacks spade grips), and the canopy supports and stern rails which are massively oversized. All these problems can be overcome with care, and a reasonable representation results. It is worth the effort as this is the only PBR model in 1:72 scale, the old Viking resin model being long out of production.

The box top artwork was copied by permission from the cover of Jim Meskoe's book *Riverine: A Pictorial History of the Brown Water War in Vietnam*, from Squadron Signal Publications. It depicts *PBR-105* in action on 31 October 1966, when James Williams won the Medal of Honor.

BARRAGE MINIATURES YABUTA JUNK
1:72 Scale

As with all the Barrage Miniatures models, this motorised Yabuta Junk is designed for over-scale wargaming figurines, 20mm in the case of 1:72 scale craft, standing on individual bases. The Yabuta needs a tiller at the stern, and a .30 cal Browning at the bow or amidships.

CALIBRE 72 (REF 72013) **LSSC**   1:72 Scale

■ This small resin kit with photo-etch from Czech manufacturers Calibre was issued in October 2005 and is currently out-of-production. It has received good reviews.

VIKING MODELS (REF VK-1011) **BROWN WATER NAVY MONITOR**   1:72 Scale

■ This full-hull resin kit which featured photo-etch sheets for the bar armour, is long out-of-production.

1:56 Scale

As with the 1:76 and 1:72 scales, at a pinch 1:56 scale models from Barrage Miniatures can be displayed together with 1:48th scale models, for example with the slightly smaller scale models in the background of a diorama. Their range includes:

BARRAGE MINIATURES LCPL   1:56 Scale

■ The LCPL is a good base for reproducing either the unarmoured or the armoured versions of the *Vedette Vietnamienne* in a scale close to 1:48.

BARRAGE MINIATURES LCVP   1:56 Scale

■ This early unarmoured version (avoid the later armoured version with oversized bolts moulded on the armour plates) can be converted to a French gunboat version or an *Engin d'Assaut*. The interior has been slightly widened to accommodate wargaming 28mm figurines on individual bases.

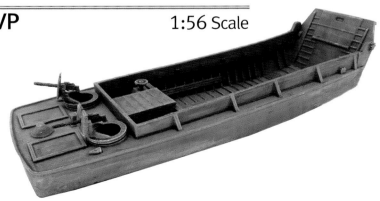

BARRAGE MINIATURES LANDING CRAFT SUPPORT Mk III   1:56 Scale

■ To produce one of the two French LCS, replace the .5in Vickers MGs with .30 cal Brownings, and the smoke mortar by a 60mm French mortar. The solid prop guards can be replaced with wire.

BARRAGE MINIATURES LSSC

1:56 Scale

■ In order to accommodate over-scale wargaming 28mm figurines, the armament has been omitted.

WARLORD GAMES LVT-4 BUFFALO

1:56 Scale

■ Warlord Games produce a 1:56 scale LVT-4 in their BOLT ACTION series, and also a 40mm Bofors, which can be converted and combined to produce a French LVT-40. This can be used for example for a background diorama shot with the larger 1:35 scale offerings.

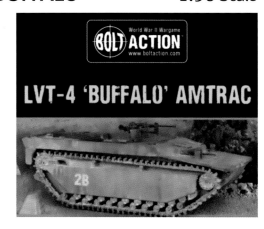

1:48 scale

MONOGRAM (REF PB179-200) RAG BOAT   1:48 Scale

■ Revell Germany still hold the moulds for this interesting model, which has never been reissued under the Revell name. Examples turn up on the second-hand market from time to time, at high prices. The Author's rare example arrived from the States with the box severely crumpled. Inside, the RAG Boat had obviously detonated a VC mine beneath the engine compartment, as the hull was shattered into several pieces. It might have been possible to convert the damaged hull back

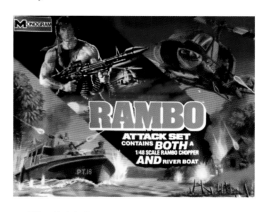

into its ancestor the 11-metre FOM, but shortening the hull and reconfiguring the bow to delete the sheer mean it is probably easier to build a FOM from scratch. The Monogram mould-maker misinterpreted the side MG shield, which is a half cylinder with one vertical slot, and a lid on top. If building the model for display on a stand, the single screw and rudder arrangement as provided was correct for the 8-metre FOM original, but the 11-metre FOM and the later RAG Boat version should have twin screws and rudders. Its serial number decal 'PT.18' is fictitious, as the RAG Boat never carried torpedoes!

The RAG Boat was also included in the Rambo Attack Set (Ref 6039), issued to coincide with the release of the second of the Rambo films. In contrast to the box lid, no figurine identified as Rambo was included with the set. The Vietnamese crew members are well-sculpted, and the 'US adviser' with drawn M1911 pistol could well stand in for 'Rambo' in uniform.

REVELL (REF 05122) PCF SWIFT BOAT Mk I 1:48 Scale

■ The second of the Monogram Vietnam Series kits, the PCF Swift Boat Mk I is still in production at regular intervals from Revell Germany. The original Monogram box lid showed a PCF patrolling offshore, but the Revell box lid shows *PCF-9* at speed, ostensibly dodging VC mines or RPGs in the Mekong Delta. The kit itself is a veteran of the Vietnam era, first appearing back in 1967.

It has a fine one-piece full hull moulding, which causes slight problems for a water-line diorama. Despite having extensive glass panels, the interior is almost completely bare. The twin Brownings in the Mount 51 top gun tub are fairly basic and are best replaced, with ammunition belt runs added. Just one single crew figure is included, although the box lid shows a gunner in the twin Browning tub. Details can be added inside the pilot house and crew accommodation. Then the moulded-on doors to the wheelhouse and crew accommodation can be cut off and replaced with open doors. The Mount 52 is simplified: the recoil protection basket should be open at the top, which will require adding a solid breech to the rear of the mortar barrel, and

the quadrants need adding to the left-hand side. The integrally-moulded mortar ammunition box at the stern needs to be replaced by a vertical-sided box, with a lid of the same size, and two fuze-setters can be added at the sides. The railings and the superstructure ladder seem quite thick, but the originals were of substantial size, and at the stern a chain is needed across the central gap. A close inspection of period photos will aid detailing work, as the railing runs did vary between early and late PCF Mk Is. To be fair, this kit – despite its advanced years – can be built into a fine representation of this attractive vessel, at an unbeatable price.

MONOGRAM YABUTA COMMAND JUNK 1:48 Scale

■ In 1967 Monogram also issued a 50-foot South Vietnamese Yabuta Command Junk *(Ghe Chú Lu'c)* in 1:48 scale, but like the RAG Boat, this has never been reissued by Revell – although the moulds still survive.

It is worth mentioning in this context that the 1:56 scale Barrage Miniatures Yabuta Command Junk comes out just slightly short of the 36-foot *Ghe Thiên Nga* Motor Patrol Junk in 1:48 scale. A deck, tiller, antenna and anchor capstan should be fitted, plus a .30 cal Browning either at the bow or amidships.

1:35 Scale

IMA (REF 10135) LCS Mk III 1:35 Scale

■ Russell Wilson of IMA (International Models Asia) in Hong Kong produces a highly-detailed 1:35 scale LCS Mk III, as a Royal Navy version. Simple conversion

results in one of the two examples briefly used by the French at the start of their riverine campaigns.

ITALERI (REF 6396) LVT(A)-4 ALLIGATOR CLOSE SUPPORT
1:35 Scale

Italeri produced the LVT(A)-4 version some years ago, converted from their original LVT-4. The turret of the kit as built has a post-war Italian internal configuration. It also lacks the armoured panels on the side sponsons.

AFV CLUB (REF 35205) EARLY TYPE LVT-4 + ITALERI (REF 6458) 40mm BOFORS = LVT-40 ALLIGATOR
1:35 Scale

With more than 460 parts including the track runs and photo-etch, this AFV Club kit of the early production LVT-4 builds into a highly detailed model – requiring a great deal of patience. The photo etch parts include four mesh sections which will be hidden inside engine bulkheads when the build is complete. A detailed crew compartment can be constructed, but unless one leaves open the three crew hatches, this detail will also be hidden. However, these features enable the enthusiast to appreciate the design of this interesting and successful vehicle, making for an enjoyable build of what would otherwise be a large floating box. The kit of the early type LVT-4 is exactly what is required to build a French LVT-40, armed with a 40mm Bofors and twin .50

cal Brownings in a large multi-angled gunshield. The two .30 cal Brownings and their mountings can go into the spares box along with the photo-etch mesh panels, but the superbly modelled .50 cal Brownings are just what are needed to fit alongside the Bofors.

Compared with the lavish box contents of the LVT, the Italeri kit of the 40mm Bofors appears quite sparse, with just 149 parts and no photo-etch. It does however build into a quite acceptable model of the US Bofors, ideal for mounting inside our Alligator. The weak point is the gun crew, dressed in hybrid American-style uniforms, but useful for furnishing four helmets. Italeri do include three Bofors clips, one for the charger and two for the loaders. The plastic gunsights are slightly overscale, and quite fragile, so photo-etch parts would be preferable. A fine metal replacement Bofors barrel can be obtained from RBModel (Ref 35B97) and additional ammo clips and boxes from AFV Club.

ITALERI (REF 6441) LCVP CONVERTED TO FRENCH LCVP GUNBOAT
1:35 Scale

The Italeri LCVP is seen here returning to its mother ship for another load. Appropriately, compared with the later issue filled with troops, the unloaded kit is just right for converting to the French gunboat version, and much cheaper. With a one-piece hull, the Italeri kit builds into a large and impressive model.

U-MODELS CONVERSION SET (REF UM122) FOR ITALERI LCVP
1:35 Scale

This set includes a 20mm Oerlikon, .30 cal Brownings and .303in Brens, plus a replacement plate for the bow, armour plating and a canopy. Note that the Italeri bow ramp lowering gear will no longer be required, which is not mentioned in U-Models' instructions.

TAMIYA (REF 35150) *PBR-31* Mk II
1:35 Scale

This is the plastic injection kit by which to judge all others, the *ne plus ultra* produced by Tamiya way back in 1999 and never surpassed. Assuredly, far more Tamiya 'Pibber' models have been built than ever patrolled the waters of the Mekong. Especially impressive are the scale thickness canopy supports, and also the comprehensive armament fit, with M2 Ma Deuces, Mk 18 grenade launcher, M60, M16s and Blooper. For a diorama, the one-piece full hull will need either cutting down to waterline or embedding in the base. One of the more attractive features is the provision of a four-man crew in realistic action poses. The crew and the very nature of the boat mean that it cries out for inclusion in a diorama, and not simply one where it is seen tied up at the quayside or hoisted out of the water for maintenance.

DRAGON (REF 3301) LIGHT SEAL SUPPORT CRAFT
1:35 Scale

This relatively small armoured craft is still an impressive model in 1:35 scale, with a full hull, and can become the central feature of interesting dioramas. Note that instead of the usual Mk 18 40mm grenade launcher, the Dragon weapons set includes the improved Mk 20 Mod 0 grenade launcher, firing the same ammunition as the Mk 18, plus three M60s. As an alternative to the armament arrangement proposed, some SEAL units dispensed with forward-firing weapons as they relied on a stealthy approach, and also to allow for rapid disembarkation and re-embarkation over the bow. One of the displaced weapons could be mounted on a new central rearward mounting, or indeed a .50 cal could be sourced for this position. A driver and

machine gunner plus four additional SEAL figures are included, in a variety of action poses, complete with a Stoner LMG, a Blooper grenade launcher, an M16, a pump-action shotgun and a silenced Beretta pistol.

SEMPERFI MINIATURES MEDIUM SEAL SUPPORT CRAFT
1:35 Scale

This limited run resin kit from Portugal is difficult to find, but builds into an impressive 1:35 scale full hull model. A SEAL crew will need to be sourced elsewhere. Note the inclusion of the original bow steps, which were easily damaged and soon replaced with a scrambling net. The top parts of the engines can be seen if one leaves open the deck access hatches, for a maintenance session diorama. However, most builders would want to reproduce a combat mission when the engine hatches would remain shut. One surprising omission is the electrically-operated Minigun normally mounted centrally at the rear of the crew compartment, to cover rapid disengagements. As several parts have been 3D printed, this impressive weapon could easily have been included.

MASTERPIECE MODELS PCF SWIFT BOAT   1:35 Scale

This large full-hull kit builds into a detailed model of the PCF Swift Boat Mk I with full interior in the wheelhouse and rear crew cabin. The box lid photo shows the scrambling net over the bow and also additional flak jacket protection around Mounts 51 and 52, which can be added. But the quality of the kit lends itself to a host of additional details to represent a specific boat, information on which can be readily found on the Internet.

MASTERPIECE MODELS ASPB (LATE VERSION)

1:35 Scale

Another excellent full-hull model, this time of the second type of ASPB, with the rear well decked over. In the configuration shown on the box lid, the rear pair of machine guns would be .30 cal Brownings. If the two .50 cal Brownings supplied in the kit are to be used, then this later configuration will also require the addition of 8 x 3.5in rocket launchers in two quadruple sets either side of the forward turret.

MASTERPIECE MODELS PROGRAM 5 'ZIPPO'

1:35 Scale

This is the specialised flamethrower version of the basic Program 5 Monitor type.

MASTERPIECE MODELS PROGRAM 5 MONITOR

1:35 Scale

Main armament of the Program 5 Monitor was the 105mm howitzer in a Mk 49 turret taken from the Marines' LVTH-6 AMTRACK. On the Program 5 Monitors, CCBs and 'Zippos' the turrets were all protected by a framework carrying bar armour.

CREWMEN & ACCESSORIES

See also the selected references on page 64.

1:76 & 1:72 scales: Soldiers in shorts are available from various Milicast and 8th Army sets, with Foreign Legion in shorts and képis from Strelets Set 187 (WW2); French hats of the 1950s from the Airfix Confederates set (Ref 01713) or the Revell Cowboy set (Ref 2554); Heads with bachis from Red Box (Ref RB72025) French Sailors of the Boxer Rebellion 1900. US soldiers, with helmets, hats and berets, from the Italeri set (6120) and Revell Special Forces set (Ref 02527).

1:48 scale: Tamiya Africa Korps Infantry Set figurines (Ref 32561); Tamiya Jerry Can Set (Ref 32510); Shapeways 1:45 scale Civilian Crewmen Sets and 1:48 scale M1 helmets. Hauler make fine .50 cal and .30 cal Brownings in resin and brass etch.

1:35 scale: MiniArt German Tank Crew Afrika Korps (Ref 35141) and German Paratroopers & Tankers Italy 1943 (Ref 35163); Master Box Afrika Korps German Tankmen Set (Ref MB3559); Figurines in shorts & shirts, with Bren Gun from the Dragon British 8th Army Infantry (Ref 6390); French képis, rifles & FM 24/29 from the Tamiya French Infantry Set (Ref 35288); French Navy bachi & FM 24/29 from the Heller French Infantry Set 1945 (Ref 81224); U-Models Indochina figurines.

Modelmakers' Showcase

ITALERI **FRENCH ARMOURED LCVP** 1:35 scale — BY AUTHOR

French armed and armoured LCVP, modified from the Italeri kit by the Author, using the conversion pack and crew members produced by U-Models, plus various figurines of Second World War Germans. And Yes, that is a 1:35 scale map of the Mekong the commander is holding.

DRAGON/MILICAST **LVT(A)-5** 1:72 scale BY AUTHOR

French LVT (A)-5, used as a gunboat on the Red River, converted by the Author from a Dragon ready-built LVT (A)-4 model, with vision ports, later turret MG armament, depression guards, bollards, antenna, and crew by Milicast.

AIRFIX/MILICAST **FRENCH ARMOURED LCVP** 1:72 scale   BY AUTHOR

French armed and armoured LCVP, converted from the Airfix model by the Author, with crew by Milicast.

BARRAGE MINIATURES **MOTOR PATROL JUNK** 1:48 scale   BY AUTHOR

South Vietnamese *Ghe Thiên NGA* Motor Patrol Junk at 1:48 scale, modified by the Author from a Barrage Miniatures 1:56 scale Command Junk. A common motif since ancient times, the eyes on the bow were meant to guide the boat through difficult times, and were copied on at least one Swift Boat, *PCF-79*. Note the recognition sign to avoid attacks by 'friendly' aircraft, a 60mm mortar amidships, the mast partners remaining from when this junk was sail-powered, and the typical anchor windlass. The towed sampan is loaded down with far more fuel than required for a patrol, so it would be best not to ask too many questions.

SKYTREX **RIVER PATROL CRAFT** 1:76 scale   BY AUTHOR

South Vietnamese RPC (River Patrol Craft) Skytrex model detailed by the Author, with canopy supports, and the stern extension which could carry minesweeping gear. The diorama depicts a Vietcong ambush, in which the commander of the South Vietnamese River Patrol Craft executes an emergency turn to starboard to avoid the deadly RPGs which can cause serious damage to his small gunboat, while his machine gunners in their cramped mountings seek out targets to return fire. A crewman caught out on deck hastily straightens his helmet as he ducks for cover behind the armoured bridge. Lacking the PBR's main advantage of high speed, the commander will be frantically radioing for close air support.

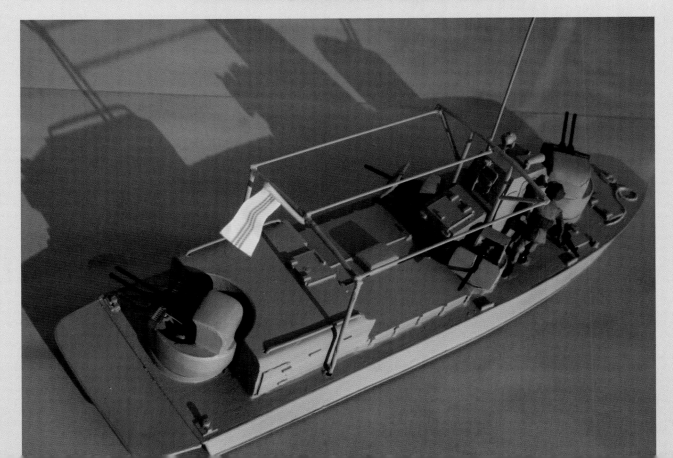

MONOGRAM **RAG BOAT** 1:48 scale

BY AUTHOR

South Vietnamese STCAN / RAG Boat (River Assault Group), a Monogram model heavily modified by the Author based on photographs, the original archives having been destroyed with the French evacuation of Saigon. The model represents the final version of the original STCAN boat (an extended 11-metre FOM), featuring the heightened conning tower with semi-circular extensions to the sides, and the late armament fitting of a .50 cal forward, two .30 cal on the conning tower wings and a third .30 cal in the rear gun tub. From photos, the side sponsons of this type do not seem to have carried LMGs.

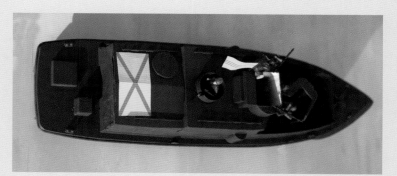

MONOGRAM/REVELL **SWIFT BOAT** 1:48 scale

BY ALEXEI PETROV

American Mk I PCF (Patrol Craft Fast) Swift Boat, the Monogram model now issued by Revell. Smartly detailed by Alexei Petrov, *PCF-38* is one option for the Revell kit, in factory-finish Haze Gray. Note the extra ropes and the scrambling net over the bows. An alternative colour reference is provided by the additional photos of *PCF-9*, shown here in faded Deck Gray overall, with the insignia of Coastal Squadron 1 which appears inside the doors of the pilot cabin. Note the blueish tint to the overall Deck Gray; the boot topping on *PCF-9* was white, and the antifouling a reddish-purple colour (Revell Ref 331).

MASTERPIECE MODELS **PROGRAM 4 ASPB** 1:35 scale BY JACK CARRICO

The 'Ambush' Diorama built by Jack Carrico for Vietnam veteran Gary Grahn, who served on *A 111-7* in 1968–69. Jack back-dated a Masterpiece Models Program 5 ASPB to represent the earlier Program 4, and included the stand-off armour screen later fitted to the front turret on this particular Alpha Boat. The stern view of *A 111-7* shows the plated-over stern well, with the .50 cal Browning and Mk 19 grenade launcher which would be fired by gunners standing in the adjacent hatches.

(Model photos by courtesy of Jack Carrico)

SKYTREX **PROGRAM 4 ASPB** 1:76 scale   BY AUTHOR

American early Program 4 ASPB (Assault Support Patrol Boat) Skytrex model detailed by the Author. The bottom photo also shows the author's Program 4 Monitor detailed overleaf.

SKYTREX **PROGRAM 4 MONITOR** 1:76 scale BY AUTHOR

American early Program 4 Monitor; Skytrex model detailed by the Author. Note the additional armour plating on the stern.

DIORAMA **PBR AND CCB** 1:35 scale BY JAN VEREERSTRAETEN

PBR Mk II with palm leaf canopy covering, carrying SEAL team members, passes a Program 5 CCB in this atmospheric diorama. Note the late design of bar armour framework around the bow turret of the CCB.

(Photos by courtesy of Jan Vereerstraeten)

MACH 2 **PBR MK II** 1:72 scale

BY AUTHOR

PBR (Patrol Boat River) Mk II. This is the small 1:72 scale kit by Mach 2, detailed by the Author. The bridge canopy is obviously a new replacement, as the crew have not had the time to paint on the white star! Note a young 'Mr T' manning the aft .50 cal, bedecked with his signature gold chains.

In the diorama the 'Pibber' crew are slowing down to pick up a downed 'Spad' pilot on the riverbank. His engine hit by

ground fire and too low to risk baling out, he has pancaked in the Mekong, and managed to reach the bank in his LRU-3P one-man liferaft. It is inspired by one of the many unforgettable scenes in the movie *Apocalypse Now*, but the Author was not prepared to saw the tail off a 1:72 scale B-52, so the Airfix Skyraider made the ultimate sacrifice.

MASTERPIECE MODELS VIETNAM DIORAMAS
1:35 scale
BY JACK CARRICO

John M 'Jack' Carrico has built several 1:35 scale Brown Water Navy models, which served as the masters for the resin kits sold by Masterpiece Models. Here by kind permission of Jack are photos of his Program 5 Monitor *M-6* with the M49 turret armed with a 105mm howitzer; PBR (Patrol Boat River) Mk I, showing the differences between the Mk I and the Mk II (the taller hull, the bridge layout and the forward gun tub); and the Tango Boat Diorama, showing a medevac conversion of an ATC, with Huey landing on the deck. The Tango Boat is built from a Masterpiece Models resin kit.

TAMIYA **PBR MK II** 1:35 scale   BY GRAEME MOLINEUX

Two views of the classic Tamiya model built virtually out-of-the-box by Australian modeller Graeme Molineux of Melbourne. The figures were inspired by the film *Apocalypse Now*. Note the surf board lifted from Kilgore, and an additional figure meant to represent Captain Willard. Details of the build are provided by Graeme at http://www.grubby-fingers-aircraft-illustration.com/pbr_pibber.html.

SCRATCH-BUILT **ATC DOUCHE** 1:48 scale   BY FACTORY DIRECT MODELS

'Irma La Douche', converted ATC with high-powered water jets, hand-crafted out of Philippine mahogany by Factory Direct Models of Phoenix, Arizona.

(Photo courtesy of Jason Wolpe of FDM)

DRAGON **LSSC** 1:35 scale

BY VARIOUS MODELLERS

LSSC (Light SEAL Support Craft) in several guises based on the popular 1:35 scale Dragon kit. The first photo is of a late configuration LSSC built by master modeller Glenn Bartolotti, returning to rendezvous with its SEAL team. Glenn has omitted the radome which risked sending splinters into the boat if hit by a rocket. Unseen in the photo are the pair of Ford V8 engines added under the rear covers. The Mekong river water is made from Envirotex Lite 2-part polymer mixed with Tamiya olive drab (*Photo by courtesy of Glenn Bartolotti and FineScale Modeller Magazine*). The fully-loaded LSSC bottom right is part of a Diorama entitled 'Wolves of Delta Part 1', by Spanish modeller Santiago Tre Calavia. (*Photo from the Blog of panzermodels.co.uk*). The other three views show the LSSC built by Matt of Black Ops Models incorporating their kits of accessories, including the fully-equipped engine bays.

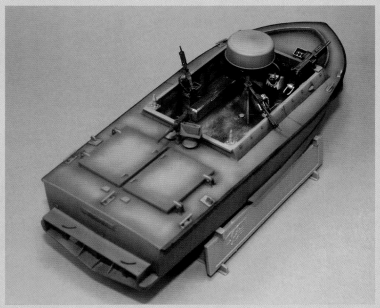

(Photos top right, centre and bottom left by courtesy of Black Ops Models)

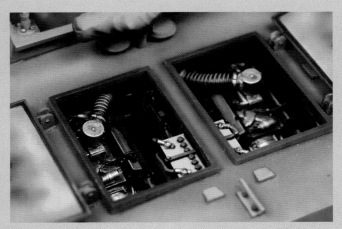

MASTERPIECE MODELS **PROGRAM 5 'ZIPPO'**
1:35 scale

BY JACK CARRICO

More photos by permission of Jack Carrico, this time showing his *Z-132-1*, the monitor armed as a 'Zippo', with two flame guns replacing the main turret.

SOUTH VIETNAMESE CRAFT

A Vietnamese Navy was set up under French auspices in 1952, but until August 1955 it was commanded by French officers. The initial establishment of 2000 men and 22 small vessels grew to more than 40,000 men and 1500 vessels by the end of 1972 when all relevant American combat vessels were transferred to Vietnam.

When the French left Indochina, they handed over to the South Vietnamese the old LCVP conversions, the newly-built EAs, the FOMs and STCANs, and the surviving Monitors and Command Boats. The Americans continued to supply LCM-6s converted to Monitors and Command

Boats, the former armed with a 40mm Bofors forward, in place of the Coventry armoured car turret, and the latter with the type of MG turret seen on the RAG Boats. The new South Vietnamese versions had a ship-shaped prow replacing the extempore

Left: A coupled pair of old armoured LCVPs, recognisable by their 20mm Oerlikons. Note the disposition of the lateral MG positions on these late-model conversions, reversed from the original configuration, and also the strengthening bars in an 'X' configuration welded on the bow plates between the angle-iron uprights. They are moored alongside an LCM-6 Monitor conversion, armed with a 40mm Bofors behind a flat gunshield. Several South Vietnamese Monitors mounted a tall multi-faceted Bofors shield similar to the turret on the later US version.

Left: South Vietnamese RAG Boat.

Below: An ex-French 11-metre FOM camouflaged for Vietnamese service.

bluff bow of the older French Monitors.

Patrolling alongside these were the South Vietnamese River Assault Group (RAG) Boats, which were a late variation on the original French 11-metre FOM. Just as the 8-metre FOM had been lengthened to improve speed and survivability, so in the STCAN version the armoured hull was lengthened to 12.4m / 40ft 9½in, and given a marked sheer at the bows, probably to avoid swamping at speed. At the same time

the armour and armament layout was substantially revised: the French .50 cal Browning armoured mountings on the FOM were very cramped, so the rear mounting was deleted and the forward one replaced by a larger gunshield. A small circular turret behind the coxwain's position mounted a .30 cal Browning. A typical French cylindrical shield on each side allowed the use of light machine guns or automatic rifles amidships. The armoured conning position

Right: South Vietnamese RPC.

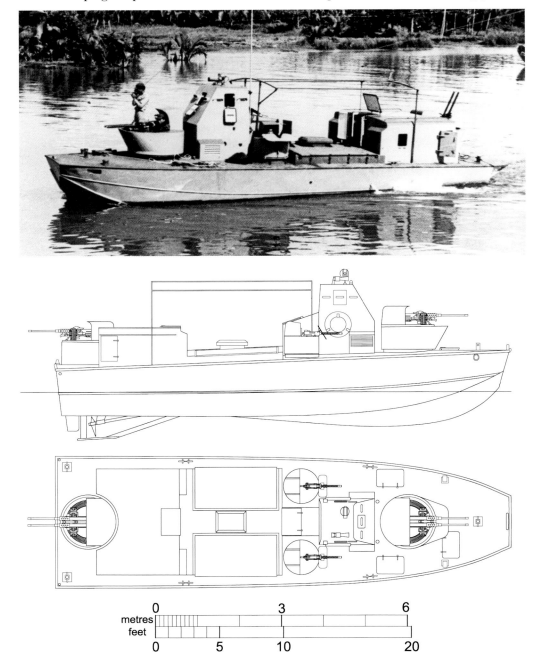

South Vietnamese River Patrol Craft

■ RIVER PATROL CRAFT

Launched: From 8 January 1965 by Peterson Boatbuilding, Wisconsin; From July 1965 by Birchfield Boiler, Tacoma.

Dimensions: Displacement 29.22 tons; Length 10.9m / 35ft 9in; Beam 3.15m / 10ft 4in; Draught 1.14m / 3ft 9in.

Crew: 6 + up to 12 troops.

Power/Speed: Twin screws; 2 x Gray Marine 64HN9 225bhp Diesel engines / 15 knots.

Guns/Armour: 2 x twin .50 cal Browning MGs in tubs bow and stern; 2 x single .30 cal Browning MGs in lateral gun tubs / Bullet-proof armour plating.

was now fitted centrally instead of being offset to port, and the cabin side armour plating was increased in height. The Americans would be so impressed with these armoured craft that they formed the inspiration for the larger ASPB.

To supplant the French designs, the Americans supplied brand new gunboats designed specifically for the South Vietnamese Navy, and supplied under the Mutual Defense Assistance Program. The order for the first ten from Petersen boat-building was completed in March 1965 and the remaining twenty-four from Birchfield Boiler in February 1966; six were transferred to Thailand in March 1967. Known as the RPC or River Patrol Craft, they were about the same size as the old French *Vedettes Vietnamiennes*, but built of steel and much more heavily armed, with 2 x twin aircraft-type .50 cal Brownings – the most popular weapons deployed in the riverine combats – plus two wing .30 cal mountings. Their light armour protection would not withstand an RPG (rocket-propelled grenade) hit, and they were felt to be too cramped even for the smaller-stature Vietnamese crews. They were slow, noisy, had a high silhouette and a poor stern design which attracted vegetation in shallow water. Overall the RPCs were unpopular with their crews and were deemed a failure.

AMERICAN VIETNAM GUNBOATS

Offshore, the US Navy and Coast Guard deployed several classes of ocean-going warships on Operation Market Time, to interdict coastal junks carrying arms and other supplies to the Viet Cong. Most drew too much water or were too large to venture up-river. One exception was the *Asheville* class of **Patrol Gunboat**, built of aluminium like the Swift Boats, and powered by gas turbines for a top speed in excess of 35 knots. Built for Caribbean patrols in the aftermath of the Cuban Missile Crisis, several of the class were sent to South

Above: USS *Defiance* (PG-95), an *Asheville* class Patrol Gunboat, running trials. *(Photo by Captain John Cost, USN, Ret, from www.navsource.org)*

■ *ASHEVILLE* CLASS PATROL GUNBOAT

Commissioned: USS *Asheville* 1966 by Tacoma Shipyard; USS *Canon* 1968 & USS *Defiance* 1969 by Peterson Builders Inc, Sturgeon Bay, Wisconsin.

Dimensions: Displacement 240 tons; Length 50.14m / 164ft 6in; Beam 7.28m / 23ft 10¾in; Draught 2.9m / 9ft 6in.

Crew: 24.

Power/Speed: Twin screws; GE 7 LM 1500 gas turbine, plus 2 x Cummins VT-12-875 725 bhp Diesel engines for economical cruise / 16 knots, total 13,300 hp / up to 42 knots on trials,

Guns/Armour: 1 x 3in/50; 1 x 40mm Bofors; 2 x Twin .50 cal Browning HMGs / Splinter protection to turret and bridge.

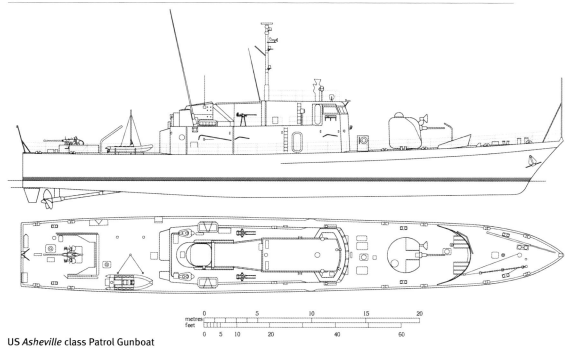

US *Asheville* class Patrol Gunboat

Vietnam, where USS *Canon* (PG-90) was twice ambushed by Viet Cong forces in the Bo De / Cu Lon Rivers. On 14 July 1971 she took a rocket hit which disabled the variable pitch propeller mechanism of her port main engine, causing her to run aground. Towed off by a pair of PCFs, she was repaired and returned to service. Then on 9 August she was hit by no less than 8 rockets, fired from both sides of the river. In the second ambush, *Canon* suffered severe damage and no less than 14 of her crew were wounded. Such attacks showed the unsuitability of using these large and virtually unprotected Patrol Gunboats in the narrow river confines.

Another offshore patrol craft, which was deployed in much larger numbers, was the **PCF Swift Boat**, developed from an oil rig crew boat. Fast and heavily armed, these all-aluminium boats were also deployed in the river estuaries and often quite far

Above: The combined 81mm mortar and .50 cal Browning mount on the rear deck of a Swift Boat. The box at the stern holds ready-use ammunition for the mortar, and the fittings on either end of the box are fuze-setters for illuminating rounds.

Right: The upper gunner of a Swift Boat with his twin .50 cal Brownings. His position gave him a good command of river banks, but at the same time left him exposed to enemy fire. Later, aircrew flak jackets and mattresses were used around the gun positions to give a degree of protection against shrapnel and small arms. Note the ammunition belt runs in trays which revolve with the MGs, and also the bars preventing the MGs from firing into the radar array. The gun tub could be accessed by a short ladder leading down into the wheelhouse, or by an exterior ladder on the starboard side of the cabin.

Below: A Mk I Swift Boat in a riverine environment.

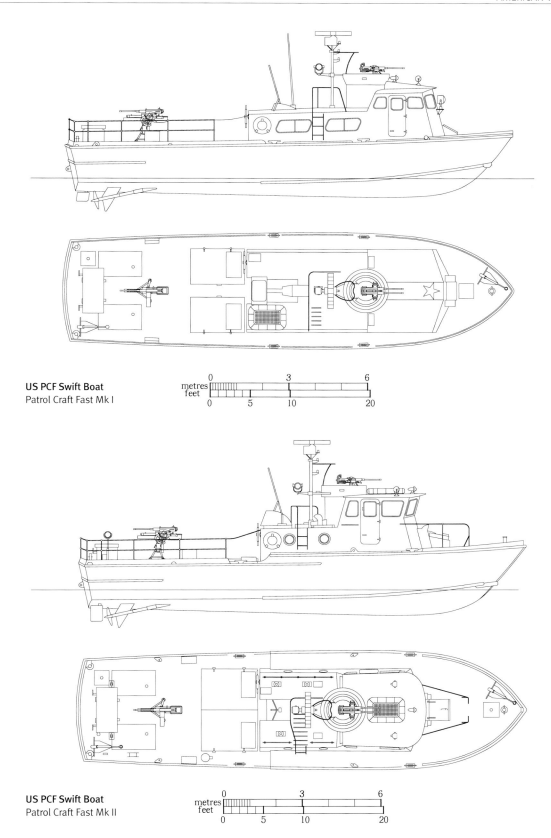

US PCF Swift Boat
Patrol Craft Fast Mk I

| metres | 0 | | 3 | | 6 |
| feet | 0 | 5 | 10 | | 20 |

US PCF Swift Boat
Patrol Craft Fast Mk II

| metres | 0 | | 3 | | 6 |
| feet | 0 | 5 | 10 | | 20 |

■ PCF SWIFT BOAT

Launched: From August 1965 by Sewart Seacraft of Berwick, Louisiana.

Dimensions: Displacement 17.5 tons light, 22.2 tons loaded; Length 15.5m / 51ft; Beam 4.57m / 15ft; Draught 1.07m / 3ft 6in.

Crew: 6.

Power/Speed: Twin screws; 2 x 12V71N General Motors Diesel engines, total 960bhp / 32 knots.

Guns/Armour: Turret with twin .50 cal Browning HMGs (Mount 51); Mk 2 Mod 1 81mm mortar combined with .50 cal Browning HMG; Forward pintle-mounted 7.62mm M60 MG or Mk 18 40mm grenade launcher / Flak jackets, aircrew body armour, 9.5mm fibreglass/ceramic plates.

Above: A pair of CCBs (Command & Control Boats) fitting out at Wilmington in August 1968. They carried the same defensive armament – here still to be installed – as the Monitors, but lacked their 81mm mortar, using its well instead for the communications equipment which was vital for co-ordinating riverine ops and air support. Note the navigation mast is yet to be fitted, and the radome mast is folded down in the position required to pass under low bridges. *(Photo NHHC 96001)*

inland. But like the *Asheville* PGs, their lack of adequate armour protection left them especially vulnerable, and from 1968 various measures were taken to add light-weight protection, especially around the gun mounting on the fantail. The early boats also proved susceptible to wave damage, the bridge-front windows often being smashed in heavy seas. A Mk II version introduced a hull with more sheer forward and a redesigned superstructure set further back from the stem.

The Americans continued to use WW2-era **LCM-6** landing craft, which were still available in large numbers. Versions which retained their original bow ramp were deployed as Armoured Troop Carriers (ATC) with spring-mounted passenger seats to protect against the shock of mine explosions, or were fitted with a helipad (ATC-

Tango) for medevac helicopters, as hospital vessels. Those intended as Monitors or Command & Control Boats (CCB) had the bow ramp replaced by a steel boat-shaped stem section, copying the preceding French and South Vietnamese vessels. At the bow, Monitors mounted a 40mm Bofors and a .50 cal Browning in a tall multi-faceted shield. In a central well they carried an 81mm mortar. On the CCB this well was filled with communications gear. The distinctive superstructure on all versions normally featured a protected coxwain's position in front of two cylindrical wing turrets each armed with either a .50 cal Browning or a Mk 18 grenade launcher. At a slightly higher level at the stern end of the superstructure was mounted a third cylindrical turret, this time armed with a 20mm cannon. These large and relatively slow

◼ LCM-6 CONVERSION (PROGRAM 4)

Launched: Second World War, by various manufacturers, converted from 1966.

Dimensions: Displacement 64 tons full load; Length 18.59m / 61ft (Program 4), Length 18.44m / 60ft 6in (Program 5); Beam 5.33m / 17ft 6in; Draught 1m / 3ft 6in.

Crew: 11.

Power/Speed: Twin screws; 2 x Detroit 64HK9 Diesel engines Total 440bhp / 8.5 knots (max), 6 knots (sustained).

Guns/Armour: 1 x 40mm Bofors; 1 x 20mm cannon; 2 x .50 cal Browning HMG OR 2 x 40mm Mk 18 grenade launchers; 4 x 7.62mm MGs; 1 x 81mm mortar OR 2 x 'Zippo' Flame guns / Plate and bar armour, total 10 tons; armoured hull sides with Styrofoam insulation between the inner plates and outer bar armour to absorb rocket shrapnel and ensure flotation.

Left: The Douche, high and dry on a maintenance barge. *(Photo by Ray F Longaker Jr, courtesy of John M Carrico)*

vessels were easy targets for Viet Cong ambushers, who were armed with heavy machine guns and RPGs, so the sides of the original LCM-6 were armour plated. Spaced away from this plating was a second layer in the form of horizontal lines of bar armour, welded to steel uprights along the hull and around the superstructure and coxwain's position. The bars were intended to break up or disrupt the hollow charge RPG warhead before it could reach the internal armour plates. The space between the two armour layers was filled with Styrofoam to guarantee buoyancy in the event of damage. Later Program 5 Monitors and CCBs also added bar armour on a framework around their turrets, but the turrets on the earlier vessels never received this reinforcement. Most vessels carried a minesweeping gear winch at the stern.

One specific 'river gunboat' version was the unique ATC Douche (known as 'Irma la Douche'), equipped with a pair of high-pressure water cannons powered by a diesel-

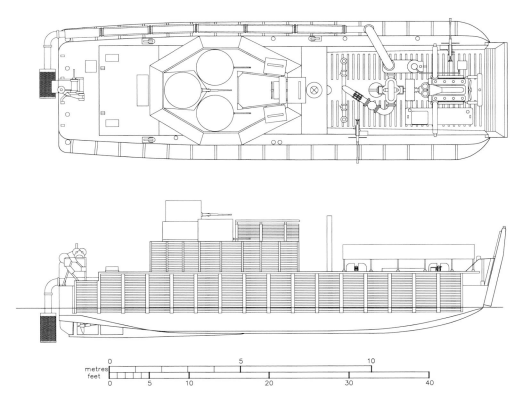

metres
feet

US Landing Craft Mechanised 6
ATC Douche conversion. In the plan view the canopies have been omitted for clarity.

Above: The 'Zippo' configuration, here on a Program 5 Monitor, carried a pair of flame guns. Note one of the two Mk 48 turrets, here armed with a 20mm cannon and protected by a frame carrying bar armour.

Above: On Monitor *M-92-2* the 81mm mortar was removed, its well plated over, and two 'Zippo' flame guns (named for the American cigarette lighter) were installed behind the 40mm turret. *(Photo by Mark Fontaine on Website http://www. warboats.org/ vietnam.htm#stoner)*

Above left: The 40mm Bofors and co-axial .50 cal Browning in a bow turret on a Monitor. Pintle-mounted .30 cal Brownings were carried at the sides of the central well. Note the lifting eye centre right, at the edge of the original LCM-6 hull. The extension to the original hull side plating is clearly visible here.

Left: Eight of the Program 5 Monitors were armed with an M49 105mm Howitzer with 151 rounds and co-axial .30 cal Browning MG with 2000 rounds, mounted in a T172 turret taken from the LVTH-6 amphibious troop carrier. Normally the turret would be enclosed in a cage of bar armour. Here the bar panels have not yet been fitted, allowing a better view of the turret. *(Photo courtesy of John M Carrico)*

Below: Close-up view of the 'Zippo' flame gun and co-axial 7.62mm MG. *(Photo courtesy of John M Carrico)*

driven pump, used not to kill enemy combatants but to dislodge them from their river bank earth bunkers. The Douche's name is a play on the title of a popular film of the period, *Irma la Douce*, starring Shirley MacLaine and Jack Lemmon.

Later versions carried a 105mm howitzer in an M49 bow turret, of the same type as mounted on the Marine Corps' LVTH-6 AMTRACK. The howitzer was capable of

firing the special M546 anti-personnel 'beehive' shell containing several thousand small flechettes. Because of its increased weight, this turret was mounted further back compared to the 40mm Bofors mount.

Much smaller, faster and more manoeuvrable, the fibreglass **PBRs** or 'Pibbers' (Patrol Boat River), were made famous by the classic movie *Apocalypse Now*, and were deployed to Vietnam in larger numbers than any other type. The result of a search for a replacement for the unloved River Patrol Craft (see South Vietnamese Section), the first 120 boats were ordered in

Left: A close-up view of the external bar armour added around the hull and superstructure. The space between the hull side plating and the bar armour was filled with Styrofoam, and usually the crew installed empty ration or ammunition cans between the bar armour and the superstructure. *(Photo courtesy of John M Carrico)*

Left: In a central well the Monitors carried an 81mm Mk 2 Model 0 mortar. The mortar was muzzle-loaded, but was normally fired by trigger. *(Photo courtesy of John M Carrico)*

Left: Note that the secondary armament on this Program 5 Monitor now comprises two Mk 48 turrets, each armed with a 20mm cannon.

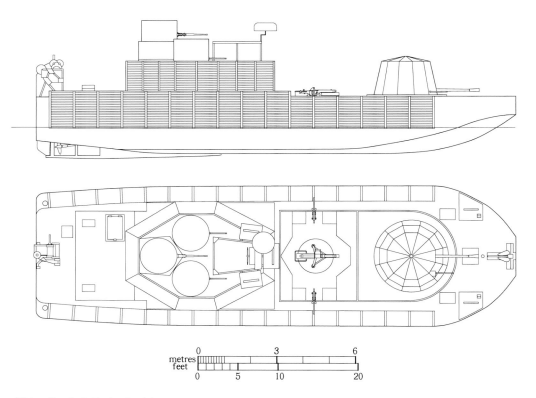

```
        0              3              6
metres ▯▯▯▯▯▯▯▯│      │      │
feet   │▯▯▯▯▯▯│      │      │
        0         5    10           20
```

US Landing Craft Mechanised 6
Monitor conversion

Below: Armored Troop Carrier *T-111-6*, popularly known as 'Irma la Douche', in action on the banks of the Vam Co Don river in March 1969. A high-pressure jet of water was used to blast the enemy out of riverside bunkers. *(NHHC K-69364)*

■ LCM-6 CONVERSION (PROGRAM 5)

Launched: Second World War, by various manufacturers, converted from 1968.

Dimensions: Displacement 64 tons full load; Length 18.44m / 60ft 6in; Beam 5.33m / 17ft 6in; Draught 1.37m / 4ft 6in (full load); height above waterline 3.81m / 12ft 6in.

Crew: 11.

Power/Speed: Twin screws; 2 x Detroit 64HK9 Diesel engines Total 440bhp / 8 knots (max), 6 knots (sustained).

Guns/Armour: 1 x M49 105mm howitzer with co-axial 7.62mm MG; 2 x 20mm cannon; 2 x .50 cal Browning HMGs. OR 2 x M10-8 flamethrowers with co-axial 7.62mm MGs + 2 x Mk-18 grenade launchers / Plate and bar armour, total 10 tons.

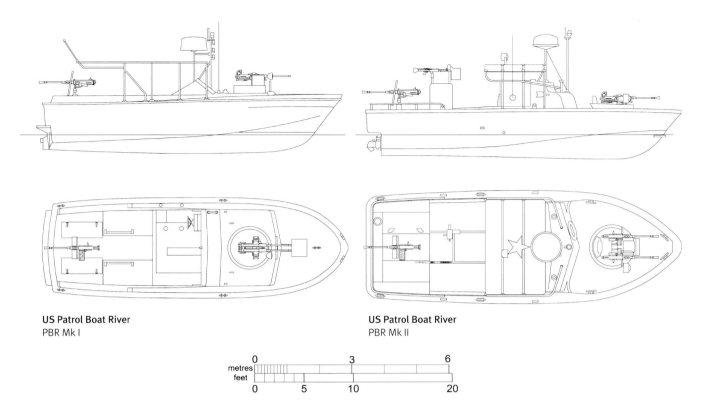

US Patrol Boat River
PBR Mk I

US Patrol Boat River
PBR Mk II

```
       0            3          6
metres |||||||||||||||||||||||||
feet   |||||||||||||||||||||||||
       0      5    10          20
```

■ PATROL BOAT RIVER

The following specifications are for the PBR Mk II. Details for the Mk I are similar, with lower powered engines and maximum speed 22 knots.

Launched: From 1965 by United Boatbuilders, later renamed Uniflite, of Bellingham.

Dimensions: Displacement 6.8 tons light, 8.1 tons full load; Length 9.75m / 32ft; Beam 3.56m / 11ft 8in; Draught 0.76m / 2ft 6in.

Crew: 4-5.

Power/Speed: Twin waterjets; 2 x GM 6V53N Diesel engines Total 216bhp / 25+ knots.

Guns/Armour: 1 x Twin .50 cal Browning HMGs forward; (on some boats, 1 x 20mm cannon replaced one of the .50 cal); 1 x .50 cal Browning HMG OR M-18 grenade launcher aft; 2 x 7.62mm M60 MGs / Bullet-proof internal plating.

1965 from United Boatbuilders of Washington State, using a militarised version of their standard 31ft Uniflite design powered by Jacuzzi waterjets. The glassfibre hull proved rot-free, and strong enough to allow beaching; it also resisted shock damage from mines and often did not set off the warheads of RPGs. However, the hull suffered from osmosis (water absorption) and the waterjets deteriorated rapidly, so the nominal top speed of 22 knots was soon reduced by anything from 2½ to 7½ knots. Armament comprised a twin .50 cal mounting forward, a single .50 cal aft, plus a M60 MG and 60mm mortar amidships; some vertical armour plate was fitted.

All available model kits depict the Mk II, redesigned to include the lessons learned with the Mk I: a redesigned forward twin .50 cal MG mount, a larger pilot house with additional armour for the coxswain, a strengthened glassfibre hull with a lower profile, improved waterjets and more powerful engines. The design maximum speed fully loaded was 27.5 knots.

More robust river patrol vessels were the specially-designed **Assault Support Patrol Boats** (ASPBs), known as 'Alpha Boats' or even 'River Destroyers', with spaced armour

and turrets. The initial model of Program 4 had some serious, and sometimes fatal, design faults: the rear deck had a well

Above: Interesting shot of PBR Mk I *No 110* of RivDiv 531, with vertical armour plates fitted for the M60 gunner behind the wheelhouse.
(Photo by Cecil H Martin on Website https:// archive.hnsa.org/ships/ pbrmkii-e.htm)

Left: PBR Mk II on patrol.

Right: A Program 5 ASPB. *(Photo courtesy of John M Carrico)*

Below: American ASPB (Assault Support Patrol Boat), also known the 'Alpha Boat' but often called the 'River Destroyer', at speed somewhere in Vietnam. This early example is armed with a 20mm Mk 16 (Mod 4) cannon and 40mm Mk 19 grenade launcher in the forward Mk 48 turret, twin .50 cal Brownings in the midships Mk 48 turret, and a Mk 2 Mod 1 combined 81mm mortar and .50 cal Browning in a well behind the superstructure. *(Photo courtesy of Al Breininger)*

Bottom: Bottom: A rare overhead view of an early (Program 4) ASPB, showing the rear well containing the 81mm mortar, which is seldom visible in most photos. *(Photo NHHC 95973)*

ASSAULT SUPPORT PATROL BOAT

Launched: First in May 1967, by Gunderson Brothers Engineering Corporation, Portland, Oregon.

Dimensions: Displacement 34.3 tons; Length 15.28m / 50ft 1½in; Beam 4.64m / 15ft 2½in (Program 5, Beam: 5.30m/17ft 4½in); Draught 1.3m / 4ft 3in.

Crew: 5 + assault team of 6-8.

Power/Speed: Twin screws; 2 x GM 12V71 Diesel engines Total 430bhp / 16 knots.

Guns/Armour: 2 turrets, EITHER Mk 48-0 Turret with 1 x 20mm cannon + 40mm grenade launcher OR Mk 48-1/2 Turret with 2 x .50 cal Browning HMGs or 2 x 7.62mm MGs + 40mm grenade launcher; Rear deck armament was Program 4: 81mm Mk 2 Model 1 mortar & combined .50 cal Browning; Program 5: Mortar replaced by 2 x .30 cal Brownings or 1 x Browning + 40mm Mk 18 grenade launcher; late modification: 2 x .50 cal Brownings on rear deck plus 8 x 3.5in rocket launchers in quadruple sets either side of forward turret / 16mm face-hardened armour plate with fragment suppression backing; + 6.35mm aluminium trigger plate spaced away from armour.

containing a combined mortar and .50 cal Browning mount, but because freeboard and stability were inadequate, rapid turns or sudden deceleration could sometimes swamp the boat by water filling the rear well, in one case leading to its loss. In Program 5 boats this defect was cured by increasing the beam, and by decking over the rear well. The latter mod was also applied to earlier Program 4 boats. Again, the armour protection of the early models was found to be vulnerable to RPG strikes, so in the later models the spacing between the armour layers was increased.

■ SIKORSKY PROTOTYPE ASPB

Launched: Late 1969 by Sikorsky Aircraft.

Dimensions: Displacement 33.3 tons; Length 15.1m / 49ft 8in; Beam 6m / 19ft 8in; Draught 1.04m / 3ft 5in.

Crew: 5?

Power/Speed: Triple waterjets; 3 x United Aircraft (Canada) ST-6570 565shp gas turbines / Up to 50 knots (as given by manufacturer).

Guns/Armour: Central turret: 1 x 105mm M102 howitzer + 2 x 20mm cannon; Remote-control bow turret: 2 x 7.62mm MGs + 40mm grenade launcher / Face-hardened armour plate with fragment suppression backing + stand-off bar armour & wire netting to trigger RPG warheads.

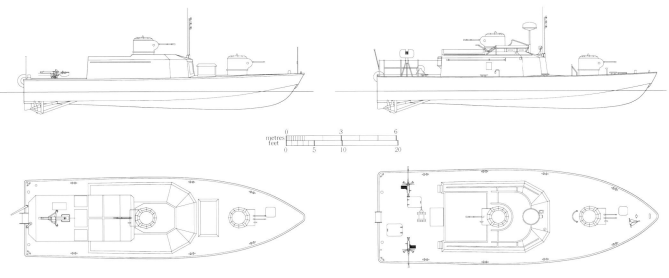

Assault Support Patrol Boat
ASPB Program 4 as designed; last boats had sponsons added

Assault Support Patrol Boat
ASPB Program 5

The original armament consisted of two Mk 48 turrets, each capable of mounting either a 20mm cannon or two .50 cal Browning MGs, plus a Mount 52 combined 81mm mortar and .50 cal Browning; this last was replaced in improved Program 5 boats with two .30 cal Brownings on single shielded mounts aft. A total of thirty-six Program 4 and fifty Program 5 were ordered, fourteen of the latter being supplied to South Vietnam.

In 1969 the Sikorsky Aircraft company – best known for its helicopters – produced a prototype of what was intended to be the first of a new breed of **ASPBs**, with higher speed and heavier firepower to outrange the Viet Cong's recoilless rifles and RPGs. Constructed of aluminium and propelled by three gas turbines driving waterjets, the boat was protected by stand-off bar armour, as on the monitors. Armament comprised a turret carrying a 105mm howitzer and two

Left: ASPB 92-7 run aground and under attack, following an underwater hit on the stern by a B-40 rocket, 14 March 1968 on the Sam Giang River. The vessel was unable to be salvaged and was later blown up by a Navy EOD team. *(USN Photo 1136903 by Navy Cameraman Dan Dodd, via John M Carrico)*

Above: The Sikorsky prototype ASPB. *(Photo courtesy of Igor I Sikorsky Historical Archives, Inc © 2017)*

Right: A SEAL team deploying from their LSSC in a training exercise in 1968. Combat experience revealed that RPG hits on the large radome could produce dangerous shrapnel, so the radome was later removed. *(Photo by Tom Hawkins from Website http://www.warboats.or g/vietnam.htm#stoner)*

Below: A rare internal view of a MSSC, showing the helmsman's position and the internal Kevlar padding. *(Photo by Tom Hawkins, on Website http://www. warboats.org/vietnam. htm#stoner)*

◼ LIGHT SEAL SUPPORT CRAFT

Launched: 1968 by Grafton Boatworks.

Dimensions: Displacement 5 tons; Length 7.3m / 24ft; Beam 2.9m / 9ft 6in; Draught 0.46m / 1ft 6in.

Crew: 3 + 6 SEALs.

Power/Speed: Two Jacuzzi waterjets; 2 x Ford 427 petrol engines total 350bhp / 30+ knots.

Guns/Armour: Various, up to 5 MGs, including 0.50 cal Browning, 7.62mm Minigun, 7.62mm M60, 5.53mm Stoner MG; 40mm Mk 18 or Mk 20 grenade launcher / Complete boat armoured to resist .30 cal rounds at 100 yards (91m) and over.

20mm cannon on top of the superstructure, with a remotely controlled Mk 48 turret on the fore deck.

However, this impressive vessel was never deployed in Vietnam, probably because by the time she had completed her trials the decision had been taken to ulti-mately withdraw American forces. It would be inconceivable to leave this new prototype in the hands of the South Vietnamese Navy, with the likelihood that she could ulti-mately be taken over by the North Vietnamese. Delivered to the US Navy in 1969, she was used to train Special Forces, and was eventually withdrawn from service in August 1980.

US Special Forces required their own specialised craft for attacking and with-drawal. They converted two LCM-6s to HSSCs, or Heavy SEAL Support Craft. Both retained their bow landing ramp, which was cut down and armoured, as were the hull and superstructure. The after section of the central well was rein-forced to carry a medevac helicopter, and a heavy armament was fitted, including recoilless guns, Miniguns and .50 cal Brownings. Their engine room was sound-proofed, and the diesel exhaust exited underwater. They were intended to be capable of extracting a SEAL team even under heavy fire, but the SEALs disliked them because of their slow speed and high visibility, features which both went against the SEALs' need for stealthy approach and high-speed extraction. Ten follow-on HSSCs were built for the South Vietnamese.

Instead of the HSSCs, the SEALS preferred to deploy using their LSSCs, the **Light SEAL Support Craft**, and the even

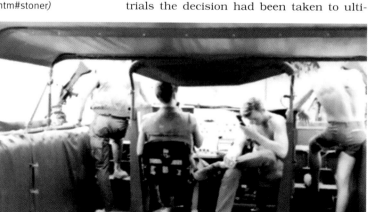

■ MEDIUM SEAL SUPPORT CRAFT

Launched: 1969 by Atlantic Research.

Dimensions: Displacement 17 tons; Length 11.05m / 36ft 3in; Beam 3.58m / 11ft 9in; Draught 1.01m / 3ft 4in.

Crew: 5 + 13 SEALs.

Power/Speed: Twin Mercruiser stern drives; 2 x 325bhp Chevrolet 427 petrol engines / 30 knots.

Guns/Armour: 3 x .50 cal Browning HMGs OR 2 x .50 cal Brownings + 1 x 7.62mm Minigun; 1 x 60mm Mortar Mk 4 Mod 0; 4 x 7.62mm M60 MGs/ Crew compartment protected by inner and outer hull with Styrofoam insulation between them to absorb rocket shrapnel and ensure flotation, alloy steel armour plating backed with ceramic, thick Kevlar flak curtains.

Above: The MSSC showing the boarding net over the bow which usually replaced the fragile front steps. *(Photo from Website http://brownwater-navy.com/ vietnam/photos2/MSSC-Long_Phu.jpg)*

Right: An LSCC coming alongside, showing its small size and what appears to be five machine guns: a .50 cal up front, a pair of 7.62mm M60s at the rear of the cockpit, and two single M60s mounted on either side.

Below: Mk 18 40mm grenade launcher fitted to an LSSC. Later boats would carry the Mk 20 Mod 0. The ammunition colours are: cases, brass; warheads, gold; links, blued steel.

Above: A factory-fresh MSSC before armament was fitted, perhaps even the very first one manufactured. The brand-new boat has the front steps which were found to be too fragile, and would be later replaced by simple rope netting slung across the complete bow. *(Photo via Jim Smith on Website https://www.boatdesign.net/ threads/help-identifying-military-36-foot-inverted-v-hull.6655)*

more popular MSSCs or **Medium SEAL Support Craft**. The latter were made of glassfibre, with an inverted-V hull form, and were fast and well-protected. Ten were ordered from Atlantic Research in December 1968.

The LSSC was built by Grafton Boatworks, the initial order comprising sixteen boats. The only significant weakness was the large radome, which made an excellent target and, if hit, would shower the cockpit with splinters.

Above: To cover a high-speed withdrawal, the MSSCs carried an electrically-operated 7.62mm Minigun mounted at the rear of the crew compartment. A .50 cal Browning is on the left. This is a boat of MST-2 Detachment ALPHA. *(Photo by Gary Hunt, on Website http://www.warboats.org/vietnam.htm#stoner)*

Selected References

BOOKS & MAGAZINES

Branfill-Cook, Roger, *River Gunboats: An Illustrated Encyclopedia* (Seaforth Publishing, 2018)

Bréchat, François, Correspondence re Vedettes in Indochina, *Navires & Histoire* N° 41, April/May 2007, pp8-9.

Carrico, John M, *Vietnam Ironclads: A Pictorial History of US Navy River Assault Craft, 1966-1970* (Brown Water Enterprises, 2007)

Carrico, John M, *Swift Boat Photo Book* (Blurb Inc, 2010)

Fall, Bernard, *Street Without Joy* (Stackpole, 1961)

Friedman, Norman, *US Small Combatants* (Naval Institute Press, 1987)

Mesko, Jim, *Riverine: A Pictorial History of the Brown Water War in Vietnam* (Squadron/Signal Publications, 1985)

Pelissier, François, Correspondence re the *1er REC*, *Navires & Histoire* N° 41, April/May 2007, pp6-7.

Pissardy, Jean-Pierre, 'Flotilles Fluviales et Dinassaut', in *Militaria Magazine* N° 17, February 1987 (via François Vauvillier, Histoire & Collections).

Stahl, Frédéric, 'Indochine 1954 : Guerre et Paix', in *Navires & Histoire* N° 41, April/May 2007, pp69-94.

WEBSITES

A.N.A.I. (Association Nationale des Anciens et Amis de l'Indochine et du Souvenir Indochinois) at http://www.anai-asso.org/NET/document/le_temps_de_la_guerre/la_guerre_dindochine/marins_kaki.html

A Tour of the Boat, by Robert B Shirley, http://pcf45.com/boat_tour/boattour.html

Boat Specifications: Mark I (PCFs 1-104), at http://www.swiftboats.net/extras/boat_specifications.htm

DINASSAUT, French Riverine Forces, at http://indochine54.free.fr/cefeo/dinassau.html

Jack Carrico's website at http://www.brownwater.net

Les bâtiments des flottilles en Indochine (1945-1954) at http://www.netmarine.net/forces/operatio/indo/

Ordnance Notes, by Bob Stoner, http://www.warboats.org/vietnam.htm#stoner

Swift Boat Plans & Specifications at http://www.swiftboats.net/extras/boat_specifications.htm

The Brown Water Navy in Vietnam, by Robert H Stoner, http://www.warboats.org/vietnam.htm#stoner

The River War in Vietnam, https://www.history.navy.mil/research/library/online-reading-room/title-list-alphabetically/r/riverine-warfare-us-navys-operations-inland-waters.html

The Tango CCB and Monitor Boats of the Brownwater Navy, at http://brownwater-navy.com/vietnam/BoatsAssault.htm

Tirilly Émile Indochine 1947-1949, at http://tirillyindochine.blogspot.com

USS *Canon*, http://www.gunboatriders.com/theboats/90_canon/pg90.html

Vedettes Fluviales en Indochine, 'Le Peleton de Vedettes Blindees du 4o/1REC', H Tourret, at http://legion-cavalerie.free.fr/ fr/tourret.htm

MODEL & ACCESSORY MANUFACTURERS & SUPPLIERS

AFV Club, for LVT-4 kits and Bofors accessories

Aires, David Lajer, for 1:48 scale resin M60 MGs & MG 151 20mm cannons, at www.aires.cz

Airfix, for 1:72 scale LCVP & Douglas Skyraider

Barrage Miniatures for 1:72 and 1:56 scale kits, Avda de Alpedrete 42, Guadarrama, 28440 Madrid, Spain. Tel: +34 915332484; Website: barrageminiatures.com

Coastal Craft, for 20mm Oerlikon models and fittings in 1:72 scale, at www.coastalcraftmodelsuk.com

Czech Master's Kits for 1:48 scale Vietnam era US pilot figures, at www.cmkkits.com.

Dan Taylor for turned metal Bofors gun barrels in 1:72 scale, and 1:35 scale mesh, at https://www.dantaylormodelworks.com

Dragon Models Hong Kong, for LVT kits in 1:72 scale & LSSC kits in 1:35 scale

Duplicata Productions, David Bruneau, for South Vietnamese & American flags and period magazines, at daveb@duplicataproductions.com

Eduard, for accessories including 1:48 scale .50 cal ammo belts, at www.eduard.com/store/index.php

Factory Direct Models, for hand-crafted models made to order, at http://www.factorydirectmodels.com

Floating Drydock for Vietnam era plans, at http://www.floatingdrydock.com/ptboat.htm

Great Little Ships, for 20mm Oerlikon models in 1:72 scale, at www.djparkins.com

Hauler for 1:48 scale .50 cal & .30 cal MGs, & scale chain, via Ilona Mullerova at pmilona@pmilona.cz

IMA, Hong Kong, Russell Wilson, at imaco.com.hk

Italeri, for LVT (A)-4 & Bofors kits in 1:35 scale

Lindberg, for LCI kits

Mach 2, at http://www.mach2.fr/index

Masterpiece Models, at http://masterpiecemodels.com/product-category/vietnam-war/

Milicast resin 1:76 scale landing craft & military models, Tom Welsh at http://www.milicast.com

Mini World in the Ukraine, for 1:72 scale machine guns, from various modelling stores

Yannis V Papadopoulos, for diorama accessories including magazines & posters, at eta300@yahoo.gr

RBModel, for turned metal gun barrels in 1:35 scale, at http://www.rbmodel.com/index.php

Revell Germany for USS *Defiance* and PCF Swift Boat kits

SemperFi Miniatures, http://www.ebay.com/sch/namsmodels/m.htm

Skytrex for FIREFIGHT 20 Series 1:76 scale Vietnam era resin models, at http://www.skytrex.com

Tamiya, for PBR kits in 1:35 scale

Tom's Modelworks for etched brass detail sets, at http://www.tomsmodelworks.com/catalog/index.php

U-Models, Rodolphe Rousille, for French Indochina models, at http://www.u-models.com